THE Father's Love and *Blessing*

WENDY THOMAS
AND LISA HUTT

Freedom Publishing

Freedom Publishing
12 Dukes Court, Bognor Road, Chichester,
PO19 8FX, United Kingdom

ISBN: 978-1-908154-59-0

British Library Cataloguing in Publication Data. A catalogue record for this book is available from the British Library

Formatted by Lucy Frankland, Freedom Publishing
Cover by Esther Kotecha, EK Design
Printed in Great Britain by Bell and Bain Ltd, Glasgow

Table of Contents

Endorsements

Every person on planet earth was created with a deep seated longing to be blessed. This foundational need is woven into our DNA, placed there by our loving Heavenly Father who blessed us at our origin with fruitfulness, multiplication and authority in Genesis 1.

It is for this reason that I am delighted to endorse Wendy and Lisa's new book on this very important topic. I highly recommend this very comprehensive resource and encourage you to read it with a wonderful anticipation of the many blessings that the Father of Lights has in store for you, your family, your community and your nation.

Barry Adams
Author of the Father's Love Letter

At the beginning of the first global lockdown in March 2020, the song "The Blessing", by Kari Jobe and Elevation Worship, was released. This song, based on the priestly blessing of Aaron in Numbers 6, spoke words of life, hope, truth and comfort to millions around the world who were living through a collective pandemic. As the song was recorded with worship leaders in nation after nation, it gained popularity and became an anthem that helped many through that time. This timely book by Wendy and Lisa unpacks the reality of God's blessing and what it can look like, both for you personally and as you seek to be a blessing to others and your world. "God is a Father who blesses" writes Wendy - this book will unpack God's blessing in new, exciting, and potentially world-changing ways! Be blessed and be a blessing...

Paul Blakey MBE
Street Angels, Christian Nightlife Initiatives Network, the
4ps.org, Faith and Police Together

"I now have come to see how the Father's love and the Father's blessing are two sides of the same coin and can't exist without each other." These words, at the start of this journey of discovery into the Father's heart of love, set the scene for an excellent review and explanation of the importance, value and power of not only the written but also of the spoken blessing. Having known the 'power of blessing' in my own life and ministry as we have prayed blessing over Scotland, I have enjoyed recapturing the joy and excitement of the Father's blessing as I have read this book - His desire to bless out of His heart of love simply pours out of every page! The revelation Wendy and Lisa have received is not only grounded solidly in Scripture, it is very personal and very practical, with example after example of how to apply the teaching in each chapter - something which is often lacking in books such as this. This will be a valuable resource to be dipped into time and time again, both by the new 'child of God' and those further along their Christian journey. Enjoy - and be blessed as you read!

Alistair Barton
Director
Pray for Scotland

'Count your blessings', was a phrase I'd heard as I grew up as a child. However, I confess I had never fully understood the power that comes from knowing the Father's Love and Blessing together until recently. This excellent book written by Wendy Thomas and Lisa Hutt will challenge, and inspire you to receive the Father's blessing which he wants to pour out upon you. This book will change your view of blessing. Counting your blessings will become a reality as you know more of God's blessing as a result of studying this book.

Adam May
UK Director of Neighbourhood Prayer Network and
Co-leader of Wixams Church, Bedfordshire

I am delighted to recommend *The Father's Love and Blessing* book. The greatest blessing is for us to discover Jesus and to be introduced to God as our loving forgiving Father. This book takes us through meditations and teaching which enliven and deepen our relationship with God as Father and with others. We are lead through a journey of reconciliation and love which heals and completes us in remarkable ways. The study encourages the reader to grow and to radically change our attitude and approach to prayer. We learn to pray blessings for individuals and communities and receive blessings as a prayer for ourselves, and in doing so to be filled with peace, reassurance and love. Wonderful.

Jenny Bailey
Director of ASK Network UK & Europe

Wendy and Lisa have made the ministry of blessing very accessible in the personal stories they share of how they have experienced receiving the Father's blessing and of how they have been led to share this in both word-crafted blessings and in practical action. May all of us who read this find that we too will revisit 'blessing' and learn to both receive afresh and then to go and share with those the Father asks us to!

Jane Holloway
World Prayer Centre, Birmingham UK

Enter into God's love
The veil has been removed

Blessing of Knowing God

Foreword

Three to four years ago, though connections with national prayer ministries in the United Kingdom, I had the pleasure to meet, quite separately, two wonderfully insightful Spirit-led women of God, Lisa Hutt and Wendy Thomas. When I recently learned that they had collaborated in writing *The Father's Love and Blessing*, I was delighted!

Autumn 2017, I was on a literal journey around parts of the UK with a friend who had previously heard the Lord say to him, Call the Nation to Prayer! I had heard of Lisa, who is on the staff of Neighbourhood Prayer Network, and I strongly felt that we needed to visit her. This resulted in an invite to stay at her home in Warrington, Cheshire. I recall an instant 'Holy Spirit' connection, as we each shared our hearts for what we believed the Lord was doing in the UK. In particular, how He was bringing His Church together, 'As One', in unity and love, both with Him and with each other.

I then learned of Wendy, who had once been instrumental in blessing 75,000 homes where she lives in Southend on Sea, Essex, with copies of The Father's Love Letter. In Spring 2018 we met, and as we chatted about God's love and His desire to bless (us) His children, I recall tears welled up in my eyes. Whenever that happens to me, I recognise it is because the Holy Spirit is speaking and that I need to listen, not just with my head, but that so His heart can touch mine.

I know that the words within this book are the product of Wendy and Lisa's own close relationship, continuous walk alongside, and attentiveness to the voice of their Father God. The wisdom so expressed through its pages, is a beautiful combination of Scripture and its interpretive revelation, by The Holy Spirit. (The Logos and Rhema Word of God entwined together.) The result, I believe, is a 'sparkling gem', and a 'bar of pure gold', a reflection from Wendy and Lisa's own hearts of the Heart of our Loving

Heavenly Father for every one of His children, whether we presently know him as our Father, or are yet to do so.

Chapter 6 contains a reflection back to the book of Genesis, to Creation, to Adam and Eve and their intimate walk with God in the Garden of Eden. Before they sinned, their lifestyle was one of blessing. They walked with their Father, shared in everything He had created and exercised His given authority over it all. That apple, taken from God's tree, lost mankind the intimate connection with their loving Father and Creator.

The amazingly Good News is that in His love The Father sent us Jesus, and through His sacrificial death, resurrection and ascension, our access to God's Creation plan has been fully restored. As the time of Jesus' final return and the restoration of *all* things grows closer, read on and discover this amazing call to a new and close, 'walk in the cool of the day' with your Creator. Knowing afresh the Father's love, each of us will then surely be prepared, equipped and energised to love and bless countless others to receive the same.

David Gilbey
UK Pioneer, The Rooftop global ministry
www.therooftop.org

Introduction

By Wendy

A good story starts with a great beginning and builds with an incredible crescendo; and so it is in the story of God's relationship with mankind and the way He blesses them. One of the first things we read in Genesis is how God blesses Adam and Eve, and throughout the Bible we hear how He blesses mankind. The Bible ends with a crescendo of blessings in Revelation where He blesses mankind with eternal life with Him and describes what life in heaven will be like. It is all about the Father's blessing.

Lisa and I wrote this course and book because God is talking to us about building a wall of blessing, with its foundation being the Father's Blessing. As we received more and more revelation, we saw how important this was for the individual as well as the nation, and we knew we needed to write both a course and a book. God is as interested and involved with the individual as He is with the nation and the world. We felt God was saying test me on this, start blessing yourself and your family on a daily basis, notice the difference it makes and write it down as a testimony.

There are established ministries that for many years have taught on blessing and we want to thank these ministries and honour them. Two which immediately spring to mind are Ffald-y-Brenin and Transform Our World. Through Transform Our World, Ed and Ruth Silvosa and their team started Adopt a Street and have been blessing streets as well as various initiatives aiming to bless people and places. So, in what way are we different?

We are talking about building a wall of blessing by declaring the Father's Blessing; this means you need to know Jesus as Saviour and Father God as your Father and to know His heart of love and blessing for yourself. We are talking about living in the greatest blessing of all – being

God's child, having a loving daily relationship with God as Father and living in His Father's blessing. This means we need to know Jesus as our Saviour, and, the moment we do, we have access to a father/child relationship with Father God. You are adopted into His family and become His child. Jesus said in John 14:6 *"I am the way the truth and the life. No one comes to the Father except through me."* Where there is a way, there has to be a destination and in this verse Jesus is the way, and the destination is Father God.

I had a dream where God asked me to drive from Lands' End to John O'Groats praying the Father's Blessing over the nation and to do this three times before driving the journey in a yellow VW campervan, stopping along the way to give out the Father's Love Letter. I have done the three journeys praying the Father's Blessing over the nation, having first asked God what the Father's Blessing was. The words God gave me are these:

THE FATHER'S BLESSING

My beloved son, My precious daughter,

You are mine and I have called you by name. I chose you before the beginning of creation. I always wanted to be your Father and live in a close, loving, Father/child relationship with you. I longed for the day you would know me that way and call me Abba, Father, Daddy or Papa. I love you simply because you are my child and I am your Father. So, it is my heart's desire to bless you.

I bless you to know me intimately as your loving Dad.

I bless you to know how precious you are to me.

I bless you to know the full extent of your inheritance and know how to use it.

I bless you to know you are joint heir with my Son Jesus and that everything I have is yours.

I bless you to know you always walk in my favour and have an open heaven over you.

I bless you to know my goodness and mercy and experience them every day of your life.

I bless you with success and to experience the fulfilment of your dreams.

I bless you to achieve the desires of your heart for it is I who placed those desires in you.

I bless you with my wisdom and to know what to say and do in any given circumstance.

I bless you to be able to hear and recognise my voice.

I bless you with the ability to hear me guide you and to follow my directions.

I bless you with my protection and send my angels to guard you.

I bless you with courage to face whatever circumstances you find yourself in.

I bless you with my peace and joy.

I bless you with my perfect love which gets rid of all fear.

I bless you to know my plans for your future are for your good and full of hope.

I bless you to know my comfort in times of trouble.

I bless you to know my encouragement.

I bless you to know how special you are and all the good things I have put inside you.

I bless you to know you are seated in heavenly places with Christ.

I bless you to know all circumstances are under your feet, you're never "under the circumstances".

I bless you to be the head and not the tail.

I bless you with every spiritual blessing.

I bless you with every good thing.

I bless you with a life of abundance.

I bless you to live a life of health and vigour.

I bless you with renewed strength as you wait on me.

I bless you to know my rest and to sleep at night.

I bless you to walk day by day, hand in hand with me knowing the fullness of my love for you and knowing your worth.

I bless you to spend eternity with me and to know me fully.

I speak blessing over every area of your life, not grudgingly but willingly, as it is my pleasure to bless you.

Love, your Dad,

Almighty God

Chapter 1
God as Father and the Father's Blessing

How I came to know God as Father
Lisa

I remember as a child saying the Our Father (Lord's Prayer) morning after morning in school assemblies. In many ways it was a prayer I did not understand, but it was my first glimpse of Father God. I became a Christian as a student and fell in love with Jesus and gave my life to Him. Not long after this, I was in a back garden at a Christian Union gathering and was handed a Songs of Fellowship Book. I remember singing the song "Father God" for the first time. The words just opened my eyes to the Father. A Father who loved me and cared for me. As the years went by, other songs moved me – "How deep the Father's love", "Father me" and "Father of the fatherless". For some reason, the words in these worship songs helped me connect with Father God in a meaningful way.

I went through a wilderness time in my Christian walk for a few years. I felt so isolated and as I spent time talking with God about everything, I began to understand that I was a child of God and a daughter of the Father. I realised that God wanted the best for me. That He had good plans for me. Things did not immediately change in my life, but as I took small steps, God worked.

Then I had a season when I was just gripped by the story of the prodigal son, and this informed my prayers and deepened by understanding of the love of the Father.

Over the years, I have been part of different prayer groups and gatherings where the Lord's Prayer has been prayed. It stopped being something repetitive and impersonal and became meaningful and intimate. I now love saying "Our Father" as I pray.

Then Wendy and I began a conversation, and out of that has come this course and book. I felt inspired to use the

Father's Blessing as part of a DIY Blessings journal which I began a few months ago and this has brought me closer to the Father. It has been such a blessing.

How I came to know God as Father
Wendy

I became a Christian at the age of thirteen and it was life changing. I immediately fell in love with Jesus. I knew the Holy Spirit living in me in His gifts and fruits, but God the Father I held at a distance. I knew He was Holy and worshipped Him, but did not think of God as Father. You see, I had been born to a single mum and did not know my birth dad, not even a name. I was then adopted by my natural grandparents. At the age of seventeen, my granddad, that I called and knew as Dad, died. So, for me I thought dads either weren't there for you in the first place or left you. Why would I want yet another dad in God? However, I was very happy in my faith and was in prayer ministry, in a youth worship group and taught in Sunday school.

This carried on for a long time until in 1999 I saw a conference called 'Ministering the Father's Love' advertised. I thought this might be helpful for others who I ministered to, so I went along. However, God met me there in a way I had never expected. In a soaking session they played the Father's Love Letter, and at the end they said if you do not know God as Father in this way come forward and that they would pray for you. As they prayed for me it was like liquid love flowing all over me, all around me and flooding inside of me, and I just knew that I knew God was my Dad. It changed everything, and was as big as a change as becoming a Christian. I prayed differently, I spoke differently, I felt differently, and I evangelised differently.

When I went home, everyone noticed a difference but when I told them what had happened, they did not understand. My mum died soon after. I know that without knowing God as my Dad I would not have got through this as well. God would have still helped me, but because He was my Dad, I could allow Him to carry me and comfort me at this time.

Since then, I have grown in knowing Him as my Dad and got to know the Father's love for me and others in a deeper way; it is central to my life and ministry. I have written many books on knowing God as Father and His Father's love.

In May 2020, God started talking to me about the Father's blessing in a new way; I now have come to see how the Father's love and the Father's blessing are two sides of the same coin and can't exist without each other. They are two sides of the Father's heart. Even as I have been writing the blessings course and book, I have been growing deeper both in experiencing the Father's blessing and understanding what it involves. It is an exciting journey that I want to share with everyone as they either read the book or take part in the course.

The Father's Blessing

Let us look at the Father's Blessing in more detail. Before we do, here are the words again.

My beloved son, My precious daughter,

You are mine and I have called you by name. I chose you before the beginning of creation. I always wanted to be your Father and live in a close, loving, Father/child relationship with you. I longed for the day you would know me that way and call me Abba, Father, Daddy or Papa. I love you simply because you are my child and I am your Father. So, it is my heart's desire to bless you.

I bless you...

> ...to know me intimately as your loving Dad.
> ...to know how precious you are to me.
> ...to know the full extent of your inheritance and know how to use it.
> ...to know you are joint heir with my Son Jesus and that everything I have is yours.

...to know you always walk in my favour and have an open heaven over you.

...to know my goodness and mercy and experience them every day of your life.

...with success and to experience the fulfilment of your dreams.

...to achieve the desires of your heart for it is I who placed those desires in you.

...with my wisdom and to know what to say and do in any given circumstance.

...to be able to hear and recognise my voice.

...with the ability to hear me guide you and to follow my directions.

...with my protection and send my angels to guard you.

...with courage to face whatever circumstances you find yourself in.

...with my peace and joy.

...with my perfect love which gets rid of all fear.

...to know my plans for your future are for your good and full of hope.

...to know my comfort in times of trouble.

...to know my encouragement.

...to know how special you are and all the good things I have put inside you.

...to know you are seated in heavenly places with Christ.

...to know all circumstances are under your feet, you're never "under the circumstances".

...to be the head and not the tail.

...with every spiritual blessing.

...with every good thing.

...with a life of abundance.

...to live a life of health and vigour.

...with renewed strength as you wait on me.

...to know my rest and to sleep at night.

...to walk day by day, hand in hand with me knowing the fullness of my love for you and knowing your worth.

...to spend eternity with me and to know me fully.

I speak blessing over every area of your life, not grudgingly but willingly, as it is my pleasure to bless you.

Love, your Dad,

Almighty God

As you can see, the Father's Blessing covers every part of your life: physical, spiritual, and mental, and it covers all your core needs such as belonging, identity, purpose, protection, and provision.

Let us now look at what God is like as a father and how to know Him as your Dad and live in the Father's blessing.

God is a father who blesses. He loves to give us good gifts and to bless us.

God as Father

How do you feel when I say God is your Heavenly Father and He loves you and wants you to live in a father/child relationship with Him which is full of His Father's blessing? I expect that will depend on the way you were parented. This influences how we think God will be as a father. However, Father God is better than the best earthly parent, so let's look at what kind of a father He is. How do you even begin to describe a father who is so wonderful? Father God is too wonderful for words to describe. You really need to know Him for yourself. He is all powerful, all loving, all blessing, just, righteous, and true. He is faithful, trustworthy, good, fair, and protective; He provides all your needs and so much more. He is everything you would want a father to be and "more than". Perhaps those last two words "more than" are the best description. When you have run out of words to describe Him, He is "more than".

If we look at the definition of love in 1 Corinthians 13, we can see how all the Father's blessings are present in the description of love. We should not be surprised at this, as we are told that God the Father is love in 1 John 4:8: God is love. 1 Corinthians 13:4-8 describes love, so if God is love we can put His name where love is written and it gives us a description of God: God is patient, God is kind, God does not envy, God does not boast, God is not proud, God does not dishonour others, God is not self-seeking, God is not easily angered, God keeps no record of wrongs, God does not delight in evil but rejoices with the truth. God always protects, always hopes, always perseveres. God never fails.

I (Wendy) wrote a piece on what I have found God to be like as my father and I hope that gives you some idea of what God is like as Father.

Picture of the perfect Father

As a child boasts to his friends about his dad and says how his dad is the biggest, best and strongest - so too I want to boast about my heavenly Dad, so that you can see just what a good Father He is.

My Dad is not just the best Dad in the whole world, He is the best Dad in the whole universe and in fact He MADE the world.

Nothing is impossible for my Dad. He can do everything. He is the King of Kings, Lord of Lords, ruler over every power and authority. He is from everlasting to everlasting, the Alpha and Omega, and He will never leave me nor forsake me.

He loves me with an everlasting love. He knows everything about me and even knows the number of hairs on my head.

He doesn't just carry a photo of me with Him like most dads, but has my name engraved on the palms of His hands.

He will never forget me. He is constantly thinking of me because His thoughts towards me are more numerous than the grains of sands on the seashore.

My Dad gives me His strength so that when I am weak, He is strong, and where there seems to be no way, He makes a way and makes things possible.

When I am broken-hearted, He wipes away my tears and collects them in a bottle and fills me with His joy. My Dad comforts me and carries me like a lamb on His shoulders. He carries me close to His heart.

My Dad's faithfulness reaches to the ends of the earth, from everlasting to everlasting He is God. My Dad performs mighty miracles and wonders. Nothing is too difficult for Him.

My Dad has legions of angels at His command and sends them to look after me. Creation declares my Dad's glory and shouts how wonderful He is. My Dad is complete love, and His goodness and mercy know no end.

He is always looking for ways to do good for me. Because I delight in Him, He gives me the desires of my heart.

Every good and perfect gift comes from Him. He gives His Spirit without measure and makes my path straight before me. He is my refuge and my fortress. He will never let me down.

My Dad is Almighty God, Prince of Peace, Everlasting Father, Father to the Fatherless, God with us. My Dad is perfect, the best Dad He could ever be and He wants to be your Dad too. Will you let Him?

Even after all that has been said about what God is like as Father, there is so much more that can be said, and I want to explain this a bit more. In the same way as in Revelation it says there would not be enough books to contain all that Jesus had done, there are not enough words to describe God as Father.

God is joy. It is part of who He is. He is the Father of joy. We are told that He is the Father from whom all fathers derive their name. Ephesians 3:14-15 NKJV *"For this reason I bow my knees to the Father of our Lord Jesus Christ, from whom the whole family in heaven and earth is named."* The Amplified Version says in verse 15 *"whom every family on heaven and on earth derives its name (God the first and ultimate father)."* The origin of the word father is 'pater', and in old English, 'faeder', meaning 'he who begets a child'. If God is the Father of joy, we were born with joy as part of our DNA. Joy is not dependent on circumstances, whilst happiness is.

God being Father of joy is also true of all the fruits of the Holy Spirit. The Holy Spirit, God the Father, and Jesus the son are all part of the triune God, so God the Father is the Father of "*love, joy, peace, patience, kindness, generosity, faithfulness, gentleness, and self-control.*" (Galatians 5:22-23 NRSV) As God's child, we too have these attributes as part of our very nature. These attributes are who God is; He is always loving, joyful, peaceful, gentle, faithful, good, patient, kind and self-controlled. For example, we are told that God IS love (1 John 4:8). We could also say God IS joy, God IS peace, God IS gentleness, God IS faithfulness, God IS good, God IS patient, God IS kind and God IS self-control.

God is a proud Father who loves unconditionally and loves us just because we are His children. He is proud of us and wants everyone to know how much He loves us. This is shown by His son Jesus at His baptism when He opened the heavens and proclaimed, *"You are my son, whom I love; with you I am well pleased."* (Luke 3:22)

Knowing that God our Father loves us and is proud of us is a comfort, a joy, a peace, a security, an identity, a purpose, and a destiny. Jesus felt these things too, and they helped to give Him strength to get through the wilderness and defeat the devil. God sustained Him. Yet we are told that God loves us as much as He loved His son Jesus. So, when we go through a wilderness experience and know how loved we are by our heavenly Father God, we too can cope and come through the other side.

There is a frustration in trying to show how wonderful God is as Father because so much could be written, and it still wouldn't be enough to describe Him adequately. You have to experience Him as your Father as yourself. The best I can do is describe what He has been, and still is, like as my Father through all my years of knowing Him well. I expect I will get to know Him even better as I go further on in my life, and in each situation I encounter He will show me what He is like as my Dad.

However, I want to tell you what my Dad is like so far. He is so wonderful. If you can imagine the best most perfect Father anywhere, then God is that and so much more. What is so amazing is He has always been my Father even before I knew Him that way. He was fathering me even when I was being formed in my mother's womb. I was born to a single mum with no father on the scene. My birth dad did not even know my mum was pregnant with me. Apparently, she did not know how she could cope with me, and so I felt insecure and rejected even in my mother's womb. As I was praying one day, I had a mental picture of me in my mother's womb and God was curled around me cuddling me, loving me and protecting me. He was being a good Father to me, even then. This made me feel secure with God; I knew I could always trust Him to protect me and love me and hold me. I am safe in His hands. Psalm 139:15-16 says *"My frame was not hidden from you when I was made in the secret place, when I was woven together in the depths of the earth. Your eyes saw my unformed body; all the days ordained for me were written in your book before one of them came to be."*

I have known God as my provider so many times, both in big and small ways. His provision has shown me what I need or want before I have even asked Him, and even before I have known what I wanted. There have been days when I have felt low or sad and, without knowing I was feeling down, friends, family or neighbours have sent me flowers or chocolates or a surprise, a card, a letter, or a gift. They have arrived at just the right time. That has been God giving me encouragement. Other times, the need has been more serious. I can remember looking in the cupboards thinking I had not got more food to eat nor money to buy more and hearing the post arrive. When I opened the post there was a M&S food voucher that was enough to buy the weeks food. It was from a newspaper and addressed to me but with no reason as to why I had got it. Again, it was my Father providing.

We have had times when we have not had enough to pay the mortgage; one of these times, we were handed a cheque by a couple who did not know us or the situation, but the cheque was for the exact amount of the mortgage. They told us that God had told them to give us a cheque for that amount. Another time, God had told us to go somewhere but we did not have the money to do so. I went to get a receipt from an old purse that was in my bedside cabinet that was full of receipts and there was £400 in cash, which was just what we needed. No one in the house had that much money and they wouldn't have known about the purse anyway. God provides in many ways. Philippians 4:19 *"and my God will meet all your needs according to the riches of his glory in Christ Jesus."*

I have shared some good things about what God has been like to me as my Dad, and I have backed them with Bible verses, but maybe I should just give a written description. God as my Dad has been all I have ever wanted in a dad. He is the perfect Father. He is constantly loving with me, even when He disciplines me. He corrects me when I am going the wrong way and gently guides me back onto the right path. He is there every second of the day. He never leaves me. He constantly talks to me and reassures me of His love and how precious I am to Him. He is always in a good mood and helps me see the good in situations and people. When I am sad, He comforts me and when I am tired, He helps me rest. He is always talking to me and also listens to everything I say. He answers my prayers. He is never too busy for me. He loves spending time with me and is always thinking of me. He is always faithful. He never lets me down. If He promises me something, He fulfils His promise. He provides for me in so many ways. He is the God of surprises, and He is always on time. Even in difficult times, He pulls me through and is there with me every step of the way. He has good plans for me and wants me to succeed. His plans for me are good, to give me a future and a hope. He gives me my heart's desires and every good gift comes from Him. He gives me what I need and also what I want. When I am unwell, He heals me. He understands me and knows me better than I know myself. He surrounds me with His love.

He sends His angels to protect me. He guides me. I have stories to illustrate all these things I have said. There are Bible verses that describe God in this way. I have experienced God as my Father in other wonderful ways also. You too can experience God as your Father in these ways. He doesn't have favourites. Just ask Him to be your Dad and show you what He is like as a Father. I look forward to hearing your testimonies.

What is your picture of the Father?

What is your picture of the Father? I love how art can help us visualise the Father's love. I remember the first time I saw the painting of the prodigal daughter by Charlie Mackesy. I was overwhelmed by the image of the loving embrace of the Father. You can view this painting and other artwork on Charlie's website www.charliemackesy.com/paintings

An invite to know the Father

You may know that China exists but have never been there. You may ask someone who has been to China what it is like? You may learn from them. But if you got the opportunity to go to China, all your senses – your eyes, ears, smell, would experience China. You would have memories from this time. Sometimes we have a head knowledge of the Father from other people we know, but we have not experienced the Father's love for ourselves. So how can we get to know the Father?

We get to know the Father through Jesus

Jesus said to him, "I am the way, the truth, and the life. No one comes to the Father except through Me. "If you had known Me, you would have known My Father also; and from now on you know Him and have seen Him". Philip said to Him, "Lord, show us the Father, and it is sufficient for us". Jesus said to him, "Have I been with you so long, and yet you have not known Me, Philip? He who has seen Me has seen the Father; so how can you say, "Show us the Father?"

Do you not believe that I am in the Father, and the Father in Me? The words that I speak to you I do not speak on My own authority; but the Father who dwells in Me does the works. Believe Me that I am in the Father and the Father in Me, or else believe Me for the sake of the works themselves. "
(John 14:6-11 NKJV)

Jesus died on the cross so we can get to know the Father as we believe and trust in Him. Jesus died so that we can have a relationship with the Father. He died for everything wrong we have done. His love is vast. He longs to bless you. To bless those you know. Spend a few moments before Him. If there are things that come to mind to say sorry for, then do so. Receive His forgiveness for you. His love. God is longing for you to know Him as Father, so it is easy to start knowing Him that way. All you need to do, if you have not asked Jesus into your life, is to do so as a first step and then simply ask God to help you know Him as Father. That might be a process, or it might happen straight away. It is a step of faith, so you have to believe it has happened even if you do not feel any change.

Below is a prayer you might like to pray.

Prayer of commitment

Jesus thank you for dying for my sins. I am sorry for everything I have done wrong and I ask you to forgive me. Please come into my heart and help me to get to know you, Heavenly Father, as my Dad. Heavenly Father, I want to know you as my Dad and live in a father /child relationship with you. I receive you as my Dad and please teach me what it means to be fathered by you. Please let me know your Father's love for me.
Amen

If you already know Jesus as your Saviour here is a prayer you might want to pray.

Prayer to know the Father

Heavenly Father. Please show me what it is like to have you as my Father. I am sorry for any lies I have believed about you as a father and ask you to show me any wrong beliefs. Please show me what you are really like. I accept you as my Father and want to live in a father/child relationship with you. Please fill me with your Father's love and show me how to live with you as my Dad.
Amen

Prayer to know the Father more

Heavenly Father,
Thank you that you long for me to know you as my Dad. This is such a blessing and I want to explore it fully. I thank you for all the ways I already know you as Father, but I want to know you as Father in the way that Jesus did. Help me to go deeper in my relationship with you. Thank you for the privilege of being your child and knowing you in this way. I love you and want to know you more and experience your blessing. Amen

Once we have prayed to know God as Father, we can enjoy the blessing of being God's child.

A Father who blesses

Before we talk about the Father's blessing, you need to know that God is a Father who loves to bless and loves to give good gifts to His children. Maybe this has not been the experience from your earthly dad, but your heavenly Father God is the perfect Father. No matter how good your earthly father was, none were perfect in the way God is. Not only that, you need to receive and live in the Father's blessing yourself as you cannot give away what you do not have.
God wants us to bless people in the same way He does. Ephesians 5:20 says always to give thanks to Father God for every person He brings into your life. God is imparting His love for His children to us, and that love means we bless them. Love and blessing are two sides of the same coin. You

cannot have love and not want to bless, and to bless means you must love the person or thing you are blessing.

We are told that God does not just love us but that He IS love. This means it is impossible for God to do or say anything that hasn't come from the source of love.

God, from before the beginning of time, always wanted His children to experience a life of blessing. This is what He provided in the Garden of Eden. An abundant life blessed by God himself. He created a perfect world and put man in it.

When God created Adam, we are told God blew the breath of life into Adam so he would have been face to face with Him, and the first thing Adam would have seen was the face of pure love, God his Father. As he looked into God's eyes, Adam would have known he was unconditionally loved, wanted, and approved of. He would have felt secure, protected and provided for. All the elements that every human needs were present, and he would have bonded with God his Father and known God would take care of him. Adam felt safe.

The very first thing He did after He created Adam and Eve was to bless them. (Genesis 1:28) *"God blessed them and said to them; "Be fruitful and increase in number, fill the earth and subdue it. Rule over the fish in the sea and the birds in the sky and over every living creature that moves on the ground.""* Previously He had blessed the birds and creatures in the sea and in Genesis 1:22 NRSV it says, *"God blessed them, saying, "Be fruitful and multiply and fill the waters in the seas, and let the birds multiply on the earth.""* The importance of a subject is shown by how soon and how often the subject is mentioned. Genesis 1:28 could not be much nearer the beginning of the Bible.

Psalm 139:5 ESV says, *"You hem me in, behind and before, and lay your hand upon me."* God the Father's hand is upon your life, imparting His love and His blessing. He wants you to have everything you need. As a good earthly father wants the best for his children, so God wants the best for you. Matthew 7:11 NRSV says, *"If you then, who are evil, know how to give good gifts to your children, how much more will your Father in heaven give good things to those who ask him!"*

Adam had all the animals for company, and he loved them. If you have had pets, you will know what companionship and love they bring, but they are not as fulfilling as good, loving human relationships. Adam was lonely, and God knew this and created a woman for Adam who could meet these needs. Another blessing. Then God blessed both Adam and Eve and their relationship. God blessed them to be fruitful and multiply and eventually they had children, another blessing. This was meeting their emotional needs.

God gave them responsibility and purpose by telling them to look after all the creation and this would also have fulfilled their needs. Then, day by day, God walked with them and talked with them in the cool of the Garden. I wonder what they talked about? I expect God told them how much He loved them and how He was proud of them. I can imagine Adam and Eve asking God all sorts of questions as they got to know each other and form a loving child/father relationship. They spent time together and enjoyed each other's company. Everything that is meant to be present in a good father/child relationship was there. After all, God is the best Father ever. You can see they were living a truly blessed life that God had always planned for them and for us.

If you want to know what it looks like to live a life under the Father's blessing, look at the life of Adam and Eve led in the garden before the fall.

God gave the perfect environment, everything needed for life. It was not dull and grey, a monotone, but colourful and varied.

The blessing of variety and colour and having our needs met.

God gave light so they could see, the sun by day and the moon and stars by night. The blessing of light and sight.

God gave warmth, that is a blessing also.

The blessing of...

- ...the beauty and variety of creation.
- ...food.
- ...water.
- ...relationships with other humans and with God.
- ...children.
- ...unconditional love from God.
- ...protection.
- ...security and safety.
- ...acceptance.
- ...unity.
- ...peace.
- ...joy.
- ...contentment.
- ...belonging.
- ...purpose.
- ...responsibility.
- ...family.
- ...knowing God.
- ...walking with God.
- ...hearing God's voice.
- ...being God's child.
- ...being made in God's image.
- ...talking to God.
- ...time spent with God.
- ...right relationship with God

Psalm 5:12 NKJV says *"For you, O Lord, will bless the righteous; With favour You will surround him as with a shield"*.

We are told that we are a kingdom of priests. In Exodus 19:6 NKJV it says, *"you shall be to me a kingdom of priests and a holy nation."* Again in 1 Peter 2:9-10 AMP, *"but you are a chosen race, a royal priesthood, a holy nation, a people for God's own possession so that you may proclaim the excellencies of Him who has called you out of darkness into his marvellous light"*. Again in Revelation 5:10 NKJV, *"and have made us kings and priests to our God; and we shall reign on the earth."*

The definition of a priest is that a priest is required to act as a mediator. He is one who represents the Divine being to his subjects, and in return from them to their God. He acts as an ambassador, a chosen vehicle through whom Yahweh God has chosen to serve the people and represent Him, on His behalf. (Wikibook definition from Hebrew)

Even more, we are God's children and should be His exact likeness as Jesus was. This means we should do and say what God says and does. Therefore, we are to bless people. We are to not just speak a blessing but to be a blessing. James 2:17 NKJV, *"Thus also faith by itself, if it does not have works, is dead."* The main emphasis of who God is, as described by God himself and Jesus, is Father. Jeremiah 3:19, *"I thought you would call me 'Father' and not turn away from following me."*

As I (Wendy) mentioned earlier, God gave me the words to the Father's blessing after He had asked me to drive from Lands' End to John O'Groats in a car, stopping along the way and declaring the Fathers blessing over the nation. I then asked Him, so what is the Father's Blessing? He then gave me the words, like taking a dictation, that form the Father's Blessing.

However, the Father's Blessing is not just these words, but is also the heart attitude of God the Father's heart as He blesses us. When we bless, it has to come from a heart of unconditional perfect love. Also, as we receive the Father's Blessing for ourselves and notice the change it makes in our life, we will want to bless others with the Father's Blessing. The Father's Blessing is a heart attitude as much as words to use to bless, though it is the words as well. Furthermore, blessings found in the Bible can be used to bless. Blessing is not just words, but also acts that bless people. You do not just say a blessing, you are a blessing.

All the words in the Father's Blessing can be traced to Bible verses as they come from the heart of God. Our parents know us better than anyone, if they are good parents, and when you love someone, you want to bless them. You know their likes and dislikes, wants, and needs and you bless based on them; it is a personal, individual blessing. God knows everything about us and knows the beginning to the end of our life. We were conceived in His heart before time began. You are Father God's happy thought, His dream come true, you fill a piece of His heart no one else can. He wants you to succeed beyond your wildest dream, and knows your wants and needs more than you do. He calls you to be who you are and delights in who you are. You are the focus of God's love and blessing; a personal love and blessing just for you. With the sharp eyesight of an eagle, God has a highly defined overview of everything concerning you and sees every detail about you. Read Psalm 139. The timing of when and how God blesses you is equally important. Timing is significant (your times are written in His book). God is not just outside of time, He sees the beginning from the end, so sees the whole of time and is over time. He created time.

The definition of blessing in the Bible is: a favour or gift bestowed by God thereby bringing happiness, the invoking of God's favour upon a person. Blessing promotes prosperity and welfare. The dictionary definition is: a favour or gift bestowed by God. Any means of happiness, a gift, benefit, or advantage. That which promotes temporal prosperity and welfare. A prayer imploring happiness upon another.

The Father's Blessing

The greatest blessing is to have Jesus as our Saviour and God as our Father and to live a life full of His love and blessing. The Father's love and the Father's blessing are both equally important and life transforming. All Christians are meant to experience them.

We have spoken of what God is like as Father but what is His Father's blessing like? His blessing covers all our needs and desires. It covers the basic human needs of unconditional love, identity, and purpose. This can be seen all through the Bible in God's dealing with people, but especially in Genesis when God creates Adam and Eve, and again at Jesus's baptism. Genesis 1:27-29, verse 28 says, *"God blessed them and said to them, "Be fruitful and increase in number, fill the earth and subdue it, rule over the fish in the sea and the birds in the sky and over every living creature that moves on the ground.""* In verse 27 they have the blessing of being made in God's image, so they knew whose they were. Then they had God's blessing which is God's favour and grace and love. The blessing God spoke over them was giving them a purpose to look after the world and all the creatures in it.   God then blessed them to be fruitful, so this is a blessing of abundance, reward, and results. They were also told to increase and fill the earth, so this is the blessing of multiplication and family. They were told to rule over the earth and fill it which is the blessing of control and fulfilment. When Jesus was baptised, He had the blessing of His Father tearing open heaven which gave Him free access to God the Father. His Father told Him He loved Him in front of everyone. This was when Jesus had not done anything to earn that love. This is the blessing of unconditional love, knowing that you are loved just because you are God's son. Then God said He was "well pleased" with Him.   This is a blessing of your Dad being proud of you and wanting everyone to know that He is pleased with you. (Luke 3:20-22.)

Earlier we have said that God the Father is love, joy, peace, gentleness, faithfulness, goodness, patience, kindness, and self-control and so these are part of the Father's blessing. The Father's blessing is all-encompassing, and one of the blessings is finding out for yourself what is included in the Father's blessing. The Bible will tell you what God is like, both as a Father and what the Father's blessing includes. An example of this is the story of the prodigal son, and we have devoted a whole chapter to this later in the book. Jesus constantly spoke of His Father and what He was like, as well as how He lived in relationship with His Father. I have previously written a book called

"Our Father" showing that in the Lord's prayer Jesus was showing us what His Father was like.

The Father's blessing communicates the character of God the Father and knowing God's character shows what's included in the Father's blessing. The fullness of who the Father is, is what gives such a complete Father's blessing. Father God invites us into relationship with Him so that we can receive His love and blessing and are able to give it to others.

Studying the life of Jesus will be a good way to see what God the Father is like and in Hebrews 1:3 we are told that Jesus is the radiance of God's glory and the exact representation of His being. Jesus himself said *"Anyone who has seen me has seen the Father"*, in John 14:9; so where you see Jesus heal you know God the Father is healer, therefore one of the blessings in the Father's Blessing is healing. John 21:25 says *"Jesus did many other things as well. If every one of them were written down, I suppose the whole world would not have room for the books that would be written"* Likewise, to try and describe God the Father and His Father's blessing, the whole world would not enough room for all the books that would be written. Enjoy finding out yourself what God is like as Father and what it means to live in His Father's blessing.

When I (Lisa) started writing with Wendy, it never struck me that I could ask for a Father's blessing directly from the Father for myself. However, I did know that the Father's Blessing she had received was to go out across the world to be shared. I was excited about this.

Yet a moment of desperate prayer on my knees led me to ask for the Father's blessing for myself. I had been studying Genesis and the image of Isaac blessing his son Jacob came into my mind. I realised if this was how a natural father blesses, how much more our Heavenly Father. Isaac had his favourite son, but God has no favourites. These are the words I wrote down as the Father blessed me.

My daughter. I call you my daughter because you are my daughter. I care for you. You do have your Father's blessing.

I bless you to know my goodness. To see goodness in others and to call it out in them.

I bless you...

...to believe in me through times of trouble.

...to receive my comfort and assurance and share this with others.

...with pictures and prophetic words to write, speak and draw.

...with a family who loves you.

...with inspirational writing.

...to share your love testimony.

...with shelter and food.

...with a love of the land and the people.

...with the joy of communion with me.

...to walk and talk with others.

...to see answered prayer.

...with discernment and wisdom.

...with an instructed tongue to sustain the weary.

...with good friendships and relationships.

...with favour.

...with open doors.

...with shut doors.

...to an international, national perspective.

...to walk the corridors of power empowered by the assignments of the kingdom.

...to speak on the airwaves.

...to hear from me.

...to speak what I give you to say.

...to see others come to faith.

...to partner for the sake of the gospel.

...to navigate treacherous waters.

...with fresh words that speak into hearts and lives.

...because I love you.

...because you are my child. Selah

Your Dad xxx

It is so easy to say God does not notice me or that is for others, but the wonderful adventure of faith is the opening up of possibilities and opportunities. Of God enlarging our understanding and growing us in the knowledge of His love and care. How He longs to bless us!

After receiving the Father's blessing, I felt I should unpack it and declare who my Father is in my life and the blessing He has given me. This is my blessing testimony. I then spent time in the Bible finding scriptures that I could pray in response to each of these blessings.

My Father

I love my Father because He is my Father. He has blessed me in so many ways.

My Father has blessed me to know His goodness. I have seen His goodness in the land of the living.

My Father has helped me see the precious in others and enabled me to encourage and build them up.

My Father has blessed me in times of trouble, being ever-present, helping me through difficulties and challenges.

My Father has blessed me with His comfort and assurance which has helped me comfort others too.

My Father has blessed me with gifts and abilities in accordance with His plan and purpose for my life.

My Father has blessed me to write, speak and draw. To be creative.

My Father has blessed me with a family who loves me. I have been blessed with brothers and sisters in Christ.

My Father has blessed me with inspirational writing.

My Father has blessed me to share my love testimony of what He has done in my life.

My Father has blessed me with shelter and food.

My Father has blessed me to love the land and to love people.

My Father has blessed me with the joy of communion with Him.

My Father has blessed me to walk and talk with others.

My Father has blessed me to see answered prayer.

My Father has blessed me with wisdom and discernment.

My Father has blessed me with an instructed tongue to sustain the weary.

My Father has blessed me with good friendships and relationships.

My Father has blessed me with favour.

My Father has blessed me with open doors.

My Father has blessed me with shut doors.

My Father has blessed me with an international, national perspective.

My Father has blessed me to do kingdom assignments.

My Father has opened doors for me to speak.

My Father has blessed me to listen and hear.

My Father has blessed me to speak from a heart moved by God.

My Father has blessed me to see others come to faith.

My Father has blessed me to partner for the sake of the gospel.

My Father has blessed me to navigate treacherous waters.

My Father has blessed me with fresh words that speak into hearts and lives.

My Father blesses me because He loves me.

My Father blesses me because I am His child.

My Father blesses me to be still and know this truth.

Maybe you would like to ask for a personal Father's blessing. God may speak His blessing to you in all sorts of ways. It may be through words, pictures, or dreams. It may be through Bible verses. It may be through the arts. It may be through music. It may be through others. It may come over time or just in one go. God loves us to ask. There may be blessings in the personal blessing above or other blessings in this book that you receive as a personal Father's blessing for yourself. Can you find verses in the Bible that are blessing that you can apply to your life? THE FATHERS BLESSING DEMONSTRATES THE FATHERS LOVE.

The Father's Love and the Father's Blessing are there for you to receive. Wendy received this beautiful letter from our Father. These words are from God to you.

My dear child

Do you know just how much I love to bless you? You are my precious child, the apple of my eye. I love you eternally and perfectly with an unconditional love. Love always wants to bless the loved one and I AM love. I want to bless you just because you are my child and I am your Father. You do not have to earn my blessings; I give them to you freely. They are a gift of grace, yours to enjoy. I say to you, freely you have received so freely give. You can bless others in word and deed the same way I bless you. I bless you in every area of life, not grudgingly but willingly. It gives me great pleasure to bless you. I love seeing your happiness as you receive and enjoy my blessings. They are one more way I express my love for you. I bless you with abundant life, not just with meeting your needs but fulfilling your desires as well. Trust me and live your life within my love and blessings.

Love, Your Dad, Almighty God

God is blessed by spending time with us

Song of Songs 2:14-15 says, *"show me your face, let me hear your voice; for your voice is sweet, and your face is lovely. Catch for us the foxes, the little foxes that ruin the vineyards, our vineyards that are in bloom."* God wants us to spend time with Him. He wants to hear our voice. He loves us, and as we spend time with Him, we can then go out and bring words of love to bring transformation.

Double blessing

God is the God of more than, and loves to bless us. Often, He gives us a double blessing. We talk about double blessing and often use it in terms of us being blessed and someone else also being blessed. E.g., if someone gives us a gift of something they no longer use but we will, the obvious blessing is to us, but it also blesses the giver, as they dispose of something useless to them freeing up space but with the joy of knowing someone else is blessed. Also, double blessing can have the meaning of an extra layer of blessing. Wendy's husband wrote her a note saying "I am blessed because I woke up this morning. I am doubly blessed because I woke up next to you". Maybe we recognise the obvious blessings we are given, but do we even look for the double blessing? Maybe we need to review our blessings.

Going deeper

Do you want to respond to God by writing Him a letter or in prayer? Are you living in a relationship with God as Father when you know you are living under His Father's blessing? If not, ask to receive the Father's blessing from Him.....

Different expressions of blessing...

- You are blessed...
- Be blessed...
- I am blessed...
- May you be blessed...
- I declare blessings over you...
- Receive a blessing of...
- I speak a blessing of... over you...

These are different ways to write, say and receive blessings. You may think of other ways of blessing.

Look up various blessings in the Bible and receive them for yourself.

Letter

My dear child,

You don't know just how good I am or how great my love for you is. My love for you never ends. It is eternal and fills the depths of eternity. From the beginning of time, I have loved you. All good gifts come from me. I continually shower you with blessings. I will always do good to you, and I work all things together for good. My plans are for your good and to give you a hope and a future. Everything I do, I do out of love. My love will cover you, protect you, cherish you, provide for you, be faithful to you and forgive you. My love means I work on your behalf. I want the best for you. My love and goodness go hand in hand and sum up who I am. I want you to fully know and experience how much I love you and how good I am because it will transform you. You will be safe and secure and at ease as you know these things and there will be no fear in you. You will no longer worry about what might happen, as you will know I am in control so the outcome will be good. You will be full of joy as you bask in my love and expect my goodness to be shown in your life. Come learn of me and live the abundant life I have always planned for you.

Love, your Dad,

Almighty God.

Prayer

Heavenly Father.
Thank you for loving me and being such a good Father. Thank you for blessing me in so many different ways. Please help me to live in a father/child relationship with you and truly know you are my Dad. Amen

Blessing

Be blessed to know God as your Dad and to live under His Father's love and blessing.

Songs

"Good, Good Father" by Chris Tomlin (2016)
"How deep the Father's Love for Us" by Stuart Townend (1990)
"Father Me" (O Father of the Fatherless) from "Crown Him" by Graham Kendrick (2008)

"Father God I wonder" by Dave Griffiths (2011)

Artwork
www.charliemackesy.com/paintings

Optional extra reading

Knowing God as Father by Wendy Thomas (2014)
Our Father by Wendy Thomas (2015)
The Father's Blessing Devotional by Wendy Thomas (2020)
The Father Loves You by Ed Piorek (1999)
Experiencing the Father's Embrace by Jack Frost (2013)
"Father's Love Letter" DVD – www.fathersloveletter.com

Chapter 2

The language of love and blessing

I (Lisa) was walking to my local shops earlier this year when I heard the words "let me teach you the language of love." The emphasis was on the words *"Let me"*. As I considered what this meant, I read Matthew 7:1-5 ESV. I was challenged to remove the plank from my eye and not judge. The words *"let me"* stood out as I read *"Let me take the speck out of your eye"* I knew I needed to let God work in the way I saw things before I responded to the things that concerned me. I had so much to learn from Him. Matthew 11:29 says, *"**Take my yoke** upon you and learn from me, for I am gentle and humble in heart, and you will find rest for your souls."*

As I prayed, I was struck how many negative, hurtful words were out there and how it was important to speak blessings. That as we did there would be an impact. I knew God was inviting me to learn from Him to bless from a heart of love and to invite others to do likewise.

What you say matters!

The Bible has so much to say about the power of the tongue and the effect of words. We could write a whole book on the subject! However, there are certain things that need to be told and Bible verses for you to look up. James talks a lot about the power of the tongue and the importance of our words and actions matching. You see, the language of love and blessing is not just about what we say but also about our heart attitude and the actions we take. I suggest you read through the book of James asking God to highlight things to you. James 1:19-20 says, *"Everyone should be quick to listen, slow to speak and slow to become angry."* It is better to listen and not speak so much because words can't be taken back once said and cause a lot of hurt. Maybe that is why God gave us two ears and only one mouth! If we can really listen to someone and hear what they are saying behind their words as well as their words, then we can know how to bless them according to their needs and know what will show our love for them.

James 3:1-12 NLT is all about the power of words and how we should speak. Verse 2 says, *"Indeed, we all make many mistakes. For if we could control our tongues, we would be perfect and could also control ourselves in every other way."*

In James 3:8-10 NLT, we are told, *"but no one can tame the tongue. It is restless and evil, full of deadly poison. Sometimes it praises our Lord and Father, and sometimes it curses those who have been made in the image of God. And so blessing and cursing come pouring out of the same mouth".* We were told that sticks and stones may break my bones, but words can never hurt me. We all know what a lie this is. I am sure virtually every person has been hurt by something that's been said to them. What sort of words are toxic poisons? Words that are negative, words said in anger meant to hurt, sarcastic words, malicious humour, humour at someone else's expense, fearful words, lies, jealous words, words said from a place of hurt, in fact any words said with a wrong motive or that are opposite to what God would say.

The last verse talks of the importance of not only praising God but praising people as well and looking for the best in them. You cannot just be loving with God and then not with people; you have to be loving with people and God, both in the way you talk and the way you act. In fact, the two greatest commandments as told by Jesus in Matthew 22:37-40, sum this up: *"'Love the Lord your God with all your heart and with all your soul and with all your mind.' This is the first and greatest commandment. And the second is like it: 'Love your neighbour as yourself.' All the Law and the Prophets hang on these two commandments".*

Learning a language

When we learn a language it takes effort, commitment, and application. To sound fluent, we will need to work on our pronunciation and practice new words. To start with we may sound different or even silly. (Lisa) I remember the first word my son said, "anana" which became banana.

The definition of language is speech or other forms of communication. An example of language is words spoken. Another example of language is words read in a book. Yet another example of language is people using their hands to express themselves. This is a non-verbal method of expression or communication, body language. We use phrases such as "we both speak the same language", meaning we understand each other because of shared opinions or values. Another phrase, "actions speak louder than words" communicates that we speak by what we do as well as what we say. In fact, there was a pop song that says: you say it best when you say nothing at all. Silence can speak.

The tower of Babel

Language is vital and words have power. When we communicate well, we unite, and nothing can stop us achieving our aims. God recognises the fact, as can be seen with the tower of Babel. You can read about this in the Bible in Genesis 11:1-9 GNT. Verse 5-7 show God's response: *"Then the Lord came down to see the city and the tower which they had built, and he said, "Now then, these are all one people and they speak one language; this is just the beginning of what they are doing to do. Soon they will be able to do anything they want! Let us go down and mix up their language so they will not understand each other."*

Language that divides

Language can be divisive, and relationships can be ended by something that was said. Whole groups can be made to feel separated by language used. The word "christanese" is used for religious language used by some Christians that people outside the church might not understand. Harsh, hurtful insensitive words can also drive people away. So, what is your language like? Can people understand what you are talking about who do not go to church? Is what you say loving, considerate and non-judgemental? We can ask God to help change our language to bless others. God forgives us for what we have said in the past as we say sorry to Him.

We are told that the tongue has the power of life and death. In Proverbs 18:21, we read how powerful our words are and the importance of guarding our words. (Wendy) My mum used to say to me if you can't say something nice then say nothing at all. Good advice.

Jesus only did what the Father was doing, so it is important that we look at the way that Jesus spoke and engaged with others in the Bible. Jesus stressed the importance of the need to feed on the word of God as well as our physical food (Matthew 4:4). He taught on blessings giving encouragement, hope and comfort. When He met the man with leprosy in Matthew 8:2 who said, *"Lord if you are willing, you can make me clean"* Jesus responded by reaching out His hand and touching him saying, *"I am willing"* followed by *"be clean",* and he was cured. You may find it helpful to study the words Jesus spoke. Some Bibles have red lettering to help us do this.

It is such a blessing to be a child of God! Psalm 139:5 TLB says, *"you hem me in behind and before, and you lay your hand upon me."* In the Living Bible the same verse reads *"you both precede and follow me, and place your hand of blessing on my head."* And in verse 3 it says, *"you chart the path ahead of me, and tell me where to stop and rest. Every moment you know where I am."* God is interested in our lives and the lives of others.

The language of love and blessing is what we should use towards God as well.

There are a number of Bible verses where we can bless God. Psalm 103:1-2 NKJV *says "Bless the Lord, O my soul;*

and all that is within me, bless His holy name! Bless the Lord, O my soul, and forget not all His benefits."

You may like to look through the Bible and find these verses and write them down so you can regularly use them.

What is language?

- relating to others
- being understood
- being heard
- being affirmed
- being instructed
- being corrected
- being released
- being identified

The language of love and blessing

So why use the language of love and blessing? When you bless someone, you do not have to agree with them. You bless them simply because you believe God loves them and wants them to experience His love and care in their lives, whether they are enemy or friend, whether you are in relationship with them or not. God desires all people to know Him. To experience His love. Romans 5:8 says, *"While we were still sinners Christ died for us."* When we live a radical life of love and blessing, the message of the gospel stands out. Others want to know more, and people come to believe and trust in Jesus.

The language of love and blessing starts with our relationship with Father God as we spend time with Him. When we receive and understand His love and blessing for us this will impact what we say, how we speak and what we do. The fruits of the Holy Spirit will be seen in our lives, *"love, joy, peace, forbearance, kindness, goodness, faithfulness, gentleness and self-control..."* Galatians 5:22-23. We are then able to share the love and blessing we have received from Father God with others as we listen, learn, and get to know them in the culture and context they are in. We are told that *"the tongue has the power of life and death"* in Proverbs 18:21. This shows how powerful our words are and the importance of guarding our words.

A dream

Whilst writing this book, I (Wendy) had a dream where I was standing in the library room in heaven. It was vast, with books on shelves lining every wall from the floor to the top. It was so high I could not see the ceiling, it seemed to go on forever. I heard God's voice say, "these are all the words my children have ever said or written. They are that important to me and make such a difference. I want you to learn the language of love and blessing and speak that, as it is the language I use and the language in heaven. It means you can speak no negative word or rude or harmful word, only words that love and bless."

This experience has changed me. Words I have used that were not swear words I now can no longer use, and I consciously think before I speak, "is what I am about to say loving and a blessing?" I do not always get it right, but I am getting better at it. However, it is the way God wants us all to speak and something I should have been doing before this dream. God wants all His children to speak the language of love and blessing. Do you speak the language of love and blessing?

After the dream I asked God how I learn the language of love and blessing. I believe He said to spend time with Him and listen to what He said as He spoke the language of love and blessing, so as I heard Him speak, I would pick it up as I let His words sink into me. This is what I am doing, and as my heart becomes full of all the words He says, I am rooted in His love and blessing and so speak those words automatically. Ephesians 3:14–21 GNT expresses this as a prayer - verse 18-19 particularly express the idea of being so full of God's love and blessing. It says, *"so that you, together with all God's people, may have the power to understand how broad and long, how high and deep, is Christ's love. Yes, may you come to know his love -although it can never be fully known – and so be completely filled with the very nature of God."*

What do you eat?

I have a question for you. What do you like to eat? I (Lisa) love pizza, chocolate, ice cream and scones! But what is it that you consume on a day to day basis? What do you read, watch, listen to and spend your time on? What we take in will inform the words we speak. Do you take the word of God regularly and intentionally? Do you hunger for it, and does it satisfy you, inspire you and challenge you? I love the account of Ezekiel's call in Ezekiel 3 to be a messenger for the Lord. He is instructed *"Son of man, eat what is before you, eat this scroll; then go and speak to the people of Israel." So, I opened my mouth, and he gave me the scroll to eat. Then he said to me, "Son of man, eat this scroll I am giving you and fill your stomach with it." So, I ate it, and it tasted as sweet as honey in my mouth."* (Ezekiel 3:1-3) Ezekiel was then instructed *"Son of man, go now to the people of Israel and speak my words to them...."* (Ezekiel 3:4) Every Christian is called to grow in our understanding of the word and to speak God's word. When we study the Bible there are so many blessings we can share with others. The word first works in our hearts so that we can speak what God has given us.

As we spend time in the Bible it is a deposit in our own hearts that builds up a reservoir of love and blessing that we can draw upon in each and every circumstance, not only for ourselves but to share with others. Listening to what God says to us directs us to love and blessing.

The words we think also matter. They have an impact on our own lives and the lives of others. They inform our choices.

A new way of thinking. A new way of speaking

Out of the mouth the heart speaks, so what we think about we will talk about. I am sure we would be embarrassed if people could read all our thoughts, so we need to think differently so that we can speak the language of love and blessing naturally in sincerity.

Finally, brothers, whatever is true, whatever is honourable, whatever is just, whatever is pure, whatever is lovely, whatever is commendable, if there is any excellence, if there is anything worthy of praise, think about these things. What you have learned and received and heard and seen in me – practice these things, and the God of peace will be with you." (Philippians 4:8-9 ESV)

We have authority in Jesus to overcome negative or sinful thoughts.

"We demolish arguments and every pretension that sets itself up against the knowledge of God, and we take captive every thought to make it obedient to Christ." (2 Corinthians 10:5)

We are called to practice the language of love. But there is a connect between what we are thinking and what we say and do. Romans 12:2 NLT says, *"Don't copy the behaviour and customs of this world, but let God transform you into a new person by changing the way you think. Then you will learn to know God's will for you, which is good and pleasing and perfect."*

Psalm 119:11 AMP says, *"Your word I have treasured and stored in my heart, That I may not sin against you."* In Luke 6:45 GNT it says, *"A good person brings good out of the treasure of good things in his heart; a bad person brings bad out of his treasure of bad things. For the mouth speaks what the heart is full of."*

Rhythm of blessing

You might like to consider a rhythm of blessing so that blessing becomes part of your lifestyle. Blessing will become a natural part of our language as you choose to bless. You may like to choose a regular time of day or a regular day in your week to say blessings over your family, neighbours and anything else laid on your heart.

(Wendy) My children are all grown now, but I still speak a blessing over them every night as I go to bed. When I have spoken a blessing over a particular circumstance in their life, I have seen a change for the better.

There may be blessings in the Bible you would like to use at bedtime with your children like the Aaronic blessing. Lisa knows a friend who did this with her family as they grew up and has testified to how precious this was.

(Lisa) As a non-Christian, when I heard the words "bless you" I liked hearing these words even though I did not understand the spiritual significance. As we use the language of love and blessing it will touch the lives of others.

Being taught by God

"But the Counsellor, the Holy Spirit, whom the Father will send in my name, he will teach you all things, and bring to your remembrance all I have said to you." (John 14:26 RSV)

There are so many good things the word of God can bless us with, and these blessings we can share with others. We are blessed to have the Holy Spirit with us who will teach us and remind us of what God has said both in the Bible and through prophetic words.

What is your motivation?

As we bless, we need to ask ourselves what is our motivation? To know the difference between blessing and flattery. In the Cambridge Dictionary flattery is defined as, "the act of praising someone, often in a way that is not sincere, because you want something from them." We are warned against flattery in 1 Thessalonians 2:4-6 where it says, *"On the contrary, we speak as those approved by God to be entrusted with the gospel. We are not trying to please people but God, who tests our hearts. You know we never used flattery, nor did we put on a mask to cover up greed – God is our witness. We are not looking for praise from people, not from you or anyone else, even though as apostles of Christ we could have asserted our authority."*

Words impact our thinking (our head), our emotions (our heart), our actions (our feet). Not long ago I (Lisa) was walking past a house and this dog ran out to me. I froze and stood still. I did not know if the dog was going to bite me. Sometimes people come across our path and they bite. Their words leave a mark. Psalm 124 is a wonderful promise of God's deliverance. It says in verse 6 *"praise be to the Lord who has not let us be torn by their teeth."*

What we believe will impact what we say. Before I became a Christian, I would routinely swear using God's name. When I became a Christian, I had a check in my spirit. Would I swear using a friend's name? I realised that God was so much more than a friend. He was my Lord and Saviour, so I just stopped doing this in my regular language.

We need wisdom to help us know when to speak and what to say. Ecclesiastes 3:7 says there is a *"time to be silent and a time to speak."* Proverbs 15:2 conveys the truth that, *"the tongue of the wise commends knowledge, but the mouth of the fool gushes folly."*

Have you ever walked into a room and there is a bad odour? There may be something in the room that is rotten. Harmful words can similarly leave bad atmospheres. We may not realise the impact words are having on us and others. What we read, hear, or see will often inform what we say or do. If we are fearful, threatened, angry or bitter it is so easy to lash out or get into intense arguments. We may have to step out of the situation to realise this. Sometimes critical unkind words are spoken over our lives. As a child of God these words have no power over us as we forgive those who speak against us, committing them to God. God wants to speak words of blessing over our lives as we spend time with Him and in His word.

Blessing, on the other hand, is a counter strategy that impacts atmospheres and changes things on earth. In the Second World War there was a Ministry of Information in the UK that regularly checked the morale of the people. It knew that this was important to help win the war. It is so easy to get depressed and cynical when we hear media reports or experience things that are unpleasant. Yet the language we then choose to use can either help things improve or make things worse. We can spread words that help or words that harm.

A need to build up others

As we look around there are so many critical words. So many curses. It is time for God's people to speak words of love and blessing. So often all we hear are negatives. We still need challenge and correction, but we need to do this from a heart right before God. Words can cause atmospheres. There is a spiritual impact of the words we speak and the words we hear. We need divine strategy to help us through the times we are in.

At this time we have opportunities to bless in new ways. There is so much fear around and as we speak blessings regularly, we will see a change not only in our heart but in the things that we are speaking into.

The words we say in our hearts and the words we speak matter. They have an impact on our own lives and those who hear them. Even if we mean one thing, people can hear another. There is a spiritual consequence.

Curses

The opposite of a blessing is a curse, so what is the definition of a curse? It is: "noun. A profane or obscene expression of anger, disgust, surprise, etc; oath. An appeal to a supernatural power for harm to come to a specific person, group, etc. harm resulting from an appeal to a supernatural power to be under a curse."[1]

(Lisa) I remember the moment when I was sat in a bar with a fellow student who turned on me and cursed me. It was horrible. A torrent of words came out of their mouth. I was not a Christian at the time. Nothing like this had ever happened to me before. I was numbed and stunned. Our

---

[1] (Collins Dictionary:

https://www.collinsdictionary.com/dictionary/english/curse)

friendship came to an end. I have prayed about the impact of these words. As a Christian I have chosen to bless that person. This does not mean that what they said was right.

Our Father longs to break the power of curses said over our lives. For this to happen we need to forgive those who have cursed us. This does not mean that what they said or did was right. But we give those words and actions to God. Jesus calls us to *"love our enemies"* (Luke 6:27 and 6:35). To bless those who curse us and pray for those who mistreat us (Luke 6:28). This is a radical, counter-cultural message. It is transformative, not only of ourselves but others. This is the good news. This is the hope we have in Christ. As we are discipled to bless, receiving the blessing of the Father, we will see God move. There is a spiritual response to our language and behaviours.

Romans 12:14-21 says, *"Bless those who persecute you; bless and do not curse. Rejoice with those who rejoice; mourn with those who mourn. Live in harmony with one another. Do not be proud, but be willing to associate with people of low position. Do not be conceited. Do not repay anyone evil for evil. Be careful to do what is right in the eyes of everyone. If it is possible, as far as it depends on you, live at peace with everyone. Do not take revenge, my dear friends, but leave room for God's wrath, for it is written: "It is mine to avenge; I will repay," says the Lord. On the contrary: "If your enemy is hungry, feed him; if he is thirsty, give him something to drink. In doing this, you will heap burning coals on his head." Do not be overcome by evil, but overcome evil with good."*

Deuteronomy 30 is where God details the list of blessings and curses that accompany being obedient to God or not. I (Wendy) love the last two verses which say: *"This day I call the heavens and the earth as witnesses against you that I have set before you life and death, blessings and curses. Now choose life, so that you and your children may live and that you may love the Lord your God, listen to his voice, and hold fast to him. For the Lord is your life, and he will give you many years in the land he swore to give to your fathers, Abraham, Isaac and Jacob."*

It is as if God wants to be sure you make the right choice. I am sure God would say in line with this, I have set the choice before you of speaking curses or the language of love and blessing which brings life. Choose to speak the language of love and blessing.

A couple of other thoughts. If you realise that every person is created by God, no matter how wicked they are, you wouldn't speak negative words but would use the language of love and blessing. They all contain something of God and are made in His image, so you should speak to them in the same way you speak to God. The way you learn to speak the language of love and blessing is to only say what the Father is saying and only do what He is doing. This is what Jesus did and how He lived His life on earth. John 14:24 *"These words you hear are not my own; they belong to the Father who sent me."*

Also, in verse 10: *"The words I say to you I do not speak on my own authority. Rather, it is the Father, living in me, who is doing his work."* You may think, well of course that's Jesus and He is the son of God, but Jesus said in verse 12: *"Very truly I tell you, whoever believes in me will do the works I have been doing, and they will do even greater things than these, because I am going to the Father."*

You can speak the language of love and blessing, and it will make such a change in your own life and those of others you speak it to. It will mean God can work more and more and bring God's kingdom to earth. Negative words are a form of curse. This has been agreed by psychologists, who will say if you tell someone they are stupid often enough they will believe it and be stupid, and so it becomes a self-fulfilling prophecy. Negative hurtful words prophesying a bad outcome for people, places, circumstances etc give the enemy an entrance and an opportunity to act and give a bad outcome. On the other hand, blessing or positive loving words calling out the good in people, places etc. bring about good outcomes. They allow God to work and bring about

His will in situations. The more you bless, the more diluted all the negatives become, and the best outcome is observed. In the end it is your choice. Will you speak the language of love and blessing and bring God's kingdom to earth? If you want to, then ask God to help you speak His language and He will show you how and make it possible. You won't regret it; it will change your life and draw you close to God and others.

If there are things laid on your heart that you have spoken in the past, take these things to God. Remember Jesus is your advocate. 1 John 2:1-2 says, *"My children, I write this to you so that you will not sin. But if anybody does sin, we have an advocate with the Father – Jesus Christ, the Righteous one. He is the atoning sacrifice for our sins, and not only for ours but also for the sins of the whole world."* The good news is we can say sorry, and God will forgive us. We can also ask Father God to help us speak the language of love of blessing.

We have written two prayers that may help you.

Saying sorry for flattery

Father God forgive me for the times when I have flattered others with my own agenda. Help me bless from a heart full of love with no hidden personal motives. In Jesus name. Amen

Saying sorry for cursing

Father God I am so sorry for cursing (a person), (a situation) or (a place). Father God give me your perspective and teach me how to bless. In Jesus name. Amen

A new way of thinking and speaking

As we recognise and realise that God is inviting us to speak the language of love and blessing, we have the encouragement that He is able to transform and renew our minds.

Romans 12:2 says, *"do not conform to the pattern of this world, but be transformed by the renewing of your mind. Then you will able to test and approve what God's will is – his good, pleasing and perfect will."*

What we feed our minds will influence how we speak. We may need to be prayerful about where we go and what we do.

Philippians 4:8: *"Finally, brothers and sisters, whatever is true, whatever is noble, whatever is right, whatever is pure, whatever is lovely, whatever is admirable – if anything is excellent or praiseworthy -think about such things."*

As we commit each day to him, Father God will help us. It may not be over night, but His love will lead us and guide us so that we can become more like him.

Testimony - Lisa

Over the last couple of months, I have been keeping a Blessings Journal. Each day I spend time with Father God, meditating upon a blessing from Him and from this place speaking blessings. I have had a greater revelation of the Father's love and how He longs to bless us, so that we can bless others from that place of receiving from Him. I have committed to bless particular people, my street, my church, and places on a regular basis. As the days have gone on, it has felt more natural and I have gained confidence to add further blessings as I have been inspired. As you practice blessing, your own attitudes towards what you are blessing change. If there are any issues, they loosen and do not have the same hold.

Imagine a glass of dirty water. As you fill it up with fresh water and it overflows, gradually all the dirt is flooded and it becomes less and less. God brings breakthrough through our brokenness. We do not need to be sorted to serve but available to bless. Our Father works in our lives as we meditate on His word, getting to know Him more. As we receive this blessing this helps us be fruitful to bless others. John 15:4-5 says, *"Remain in me, as I also remain in you. No branch can bear fruit by itself; it must remain in the vine.*

Neither can you bear fruit unless you remain in me. I am the vine; you are the branches. If you remain in me and I in you, you will bear much fruit; apart from me you can do nothing."

Even in tough times, as we meditate on the words in the Bible, we have the promise that even then that God will bless us.

Psalm 1:1-3 says, *"Blessed is the one who does not walk in step with the wicked or stand in the way that sinners take or sit in the company of mockers, but whose delight is in the law of the LORD, and who meditates on his law day and night. That person is like a tree planted by streams of water, which yields its fruit in season and whose leaf does not wither— whatever they do prospers.* We are blessed to know that our Father, *"watches over the way of the righteous."* (Psalm 1:6)

In the times we are in, we can receive the blessing of being strengthened in our inner being by the Father. Ephesians 3:16 says, *"I pray that out of his glorious riches he may strengthen you with power through his Spirit in your inner being.".* In the Amplified Version it goes further saying*: "May He grant you out of the rich treasury of His glory to be strengthened and reinforced with mighty power in the inner man by the [Holy] Spirit [Himself indwelling your innermost being and personality]." May Christ through your faith [actually] dwell (settle down, abide, make His permanent home) in your hearts! May you be rooted deep in love and founded securely on love, That you may have the power and be strong to apprehend and grasp with all the saints [God's devoted people, the experience of that love] what is the breadth and length and height and depth [of it]; [That you may really come] to know [practically, through experience for yourselves] the love of Christ, which far surpasses mere knowledge [without experience]; that you may be filled [through all your being] unto all the fullness of God [may have the richest measure of the divine Presence, and become a body wholly filled and flooded with God Himself]!* (Ephesians 3:16-19 AMP) As I prayerfully considered what the treasury of His glory was, I realised that it was the Father's love and blessing for us, so we can be rooted and experience His love, expressing this in practical ways to support and care for each other and others.

Going deeper

Questions for going deeper

- Are you more aware of the language you use, and the language others speak?
- Do you think that what you say or what others say matters?
- In your typical day where would you hear or read words that are blessings or curses?
- What is the difference between flattery and blessing?
- What is the difference between a curse and a blessing?
- Have you ever tried to learn another language?
- Did you find it hard to learn another language?

Letter

My dear child,

You have no idea how I long for my children to talk the language of love and blessing to each other. Language streaming from a heart of love because out of what is in your heart comes the words you say. You need to receive my love and blessing continually, for when your heart is full of them you will naturally speak words of love and blessing. I want you to speak from the overflow, not dredging around for loving words that leave you feeling drained. Be continually filled with my Holy Spirit and spend time with me. I always speak from a heart of love, so the more you listen to my language the more you will speak likewise. Words have the power of life and death, so choose to speak life-giving words, words of love and encouragement. Speak to others the way you speak to me and be full of loving kindness,

Love, Your Dad, Almighty God

Prayer

Heavenly Father thank you for everything you have spoken to us today. Please help us learn the language of love and blessing and stop using negative words. Remind us when we slip into our old habits and use wrong language. Father, we pray that we can listen to you and hear you use the words of love and blessing to us, so that we can learn them from you. Please bless us all as we go throughout the week and keep speaking to us. Amen

Blessing

Be blessed to speak only the language of love and blessing and have that language spoken to you.

Songs

The Blessing with Cody Carnes, Elevation worship and Kari Jobe (2020)
The Heart of the Father – Ryan Ellis, Elevation worship (2021)

Optional extra reading

The Father's Blessing Devotional by Wendy Thomas *(2020)*
Daddy you love me by Brent Lokker (2012)

Chapter 3

Obstacles to blessing

God always wants to bless us and there are some blessings He gives that are not dependant on us. In Matthew 5:45 we are told, *"he causes his sun to rise on the evil and the good, and sends rain on the righteous and the unrighteous."* Both the sun and rain are blessings freely given to all. However, though God is always willing to give His blessings, we have to receive them. There are things that make it hard to receive His blessing. This is because things can be an obstacle to our closeness to God and sometimes we are blinded so we can't see God's blessings and enjoy and receive them. Once we know what those obstacles are, we can get rid of them with God's help! Did you understand that? Even though it is us who puts the obstacles there, God is so keen to bless us that He helps us get rid of the obstacles. He certainly is a good Father God. Settle down and learn what obstacles there are, so you can get rid of them and live a life under your Father's blessing.

The enemy does not want us to receive God's blessings, but he has not the same strength and authority as God; he has already lost the battle and we have authority over him rather than the other way round. That is why we need to know the blessings God has given us, receive them into our lives and tell the enemy "hands off!"

It is as if for each one of us God has a treasure chest that is huge and overflowing with His love and blessings, like precious jewels. The lid is open, and the jewels (blessings) are overflowing. We just have to receive them. We are told in Ephesians 1:3 that, *"Praise be to the God and Father of our Lord Jesus Christ, who has blessed us in the heavenly realms with **every spiritual blessing** in Christ."* Think about that. Every spiritual blessing.... that means nothing is missing or lacking and there is the abundant life God always intended for us.

Spiritual blessings

Spiritual blessings are all that God the Father has for us and all that God the Father is. This would include the gifts of the Holy Spirit that are found in 1 Corinthians 12:1-31 and the fruit of the Holy Spirit that are found in Galatians 5:22-23. Spiritual blessings are everything that is found in heaven that can be brought to earth, so His kingdom comes to earth. The ultimate spiritual blessing is spending time with the Father and knowing His love for you and for others. The word blessing in Greek is 'eulogia', which translates "benefit". When we use the phrase 'spiritual benefits', it helps us understand the importance of receiving the benefits Father God has for us and of sharing these benefits with others.

However, we do put obstacles to receiving and giving blessings. Let's look at obstacles to us receiving blessings first.

Not recognising blessings

(Wendy) Sometimes we just do not recognise God's blessings and therefore do not receive them. A while back, I went out for the day with our son and granddaughter who was then only twenty months old. She enjoyed everything, though she would not have known they were blessings. I could have taken it for granted, or at most just thought that it was a nice day out, but I recognised the blessings. I saw the blessing of spending time with family. I saw the blessing of being out in the open and somewhere different (I had never been there before). I saw the blessing of it being dry. The forecast had been for rain, but I asked God for dry weather and that was what we had. As most things were in the open this was a blessing. I saw the blessing of enjoying being with my family. I saw the blessing of time spent together. If we do not recognise something as a blessing, we aren't as blessed by it.

Imagine a child being given one gift at a time with a heap of presents nearby unopened. The child did not appear to notice the other gifts but took that one gift and went and played with it. The heap of presents was still there but they were forgotten. In many ways we too can receive a blessing and not realise there are so many other blessings available for us. Ask Father God if there are blessings that you have not yet received that are there for you.

If you do not know what the Father's blessings are, you cannot receive His blessings for you. God is wanting to take your blinkers off. It is like having a mask over your eyes, meaning that you cannot see anything. We need to take the mask off, so we are able to see and receive God's blessings.

We have already mentioned that the word blessing in Greek is 'eulogia' which translates to 'benefit'. Psalm 103:1-2 NKJV says, *"Bless the Lord, O my soul; and all that is within me, bless His holy name! Bless the Lord, O my soul, and forget not all His benefits"* If we take the word 'benefits' in Psalm 103:1 NKJV and replace it with 'blessings' it reads, *"Bless the Lord, O my soul; and all that is within me, bless His holy name! Bless the Lord, O my soul, and forget not all His <u>blessings</u>"*. This gives us an insight into how important it is to not forget all God has done for us. Lamentations 3:21-23 says, *"Yet this I call to mind and therefore I have hope: Because of the Lord's great love we are not consumed, for his compassions never fail. They are new every morning; great is your faithfulness."* We are also not to forget God's character and who He is. It is not just about receiving blessings, but also the blessing of God himself and knowing that He is with us each day. There are so many blessings we can recognise and receive when we take the time to remember who God is and all He has done.

There was an old song that went "Count your blessings, name them one by one. Count your blessings, see what God has done"[2].

We can also receive unexpected blessings. Both of us have had neighbours give us flowers which has been so

---

[2] Johnson Oatman (1897)

lovely. Maybe you can think of times people have blessed you unexpectedly. Thank God for these blessings.

Not being grateful

We are told to be grateful for everything in many places but 1 Thessalonians 5:18 NLT says, *"be thankful in all circumstances, for this is God's will for those of you who belong to Christ Jesus."* Not being grateful means we aren't recognising the many blessings God gives us and this stops us from receiving more. The above verse says to be thankful in all circumstances, so not just in the good times. There is always something to be thankful for, even in the worst circumstances, such as the fact God loves us and is with us. Also, we need to be thankful for all people. 1 Timothy 2:1-2 says, *"I urge, then, first of all, that petitions, prayers, intercession and thanksgiving be made for all people – for kings and all those in authority, that we may live peaceful and quiet lives in all godliness and holiness."* It is easy to be thankful for some people, but God created everyone and so we should be grateful for everyone.

God does not make rubbish, so everyone is valuable. We just need to see them through God's eyes. If we are not grateful, we will not think to thank God. We may find it hard to appreciate all the blessings He has for us. Our attitude can impact our gratitude to Him for being there with us through every trial and tribulation. Our Father is there with us as we pour out our hearts to Him. We are told to *"not be anxious about anything, but in every situation, by prayer and petition, with thanksgiving, present your requests to God. And the peace of God, which transcends all understanding, will guard your hearts and your minds in Christ Jesus."* (Philippians 4:6-7) What an amazing promise! The blessing of peace that passes all understanding. This is good news to a world that is hurting and stressed.

Not listening to God and others

Listening is more than just hearing what is said. It is hearing the heart and meaning behind the words. Feeling the emotions behind the words. If we do not listen to God, then we do not hear what He wants us to do, and we miss out on the accompanying blessings. God often uses other people to speak to us and when we don't listen to others, we miss out on what God is saying.

When we do not listen to God and hear from Him in whatever way, we do we miss so much. Whether it is through the Bible, the peace in our heart as we invite Him into the decisions we make, or the counsel of others who we trust.

Low self esteem

Low self-esteem can keep us from receiving all the blessings God has for us. We may think that God could not possibly care for us, or that we have made so many mistakes God will not bless us. We may struggle to receive encouragement from others if we have a low opinion of ourselves. Yet our Father God is there to bless us, and He wants us to receive encouragements from those who He brings across our path, and through His word. He has good things to say about us. (Lisa) I remember God gently challenging me about my own low self-esteem. I had the words "I esteem you highly, it is self that gets in the way." I realised that I was holding a negative mirror of my own making. I can so easily forget how much Father God loves me. In Romans 1:25, we are encouraged to listen and apply the word of God. When we grow in our understanding of how much our Father loves us, we are then able to bless others in what we say and do.

Unworthiness

A feeling of unworthiness may hinder us receiving the blessings our Father has for us. When we grasp that Jesus died on the cross so we can have a relationship with our Father, that everyone is unworthy but because of Jesus we are made worthy, we can receive every good gift our Father has for us. James 1:17 says, *"Every good and perfect gift is from above, coming down from the Father of the heavenly lights, who does not change like shifting shadows."*

Self-worth

Self-worth is knowing you are loved and important. The second most important commandment is to love your neighbour as yourself (Matthew 22:37); this shows you will only love your neighbour to the extent you love yourself. This applies to blessing as well. If you do not receive God's blessing for yourself, you will not be able to bless others. If you do not feel worthy of God's blessings, then you will not ask for them or receive them. God is ready and waiting to bless you, you just have to ask Him for the blessings. God wants to bless you just because you are His child, and He loves you. You do not have to earn God's blessings. They are yours because Jesus died for you, so you can become God's child and receive everything God has, which includes EVERY blessing. You are so important to God that He sent His son to die for you so you could be part of His family and live with Him.

Sometimes we are held back from receiving blessing because of things we have done in the past, or things that people have done to us. We can think that we are not worthy of God's blessing. Yet God longs to bless us and help us write new chapters in our lives where we receive all He has for us, coming into our identity in Him as God's child so we can then overflow with God's love. God can also work in your story to use previous chapters for good. God can heal and restore you and give you back the years the locusts have eaten. Give the past to God and let Him deal with it as He wills.

These are some scriptures about how God sees you

As you read through these scriptures apply them to yourself.

I am fearfully and wonderfully made – Psalm 139:14
God thinks of me constantly – Psalm 139:17
God cherishes me – Psalm 139:18
God formed me – Psalm 139:15
God wove me together in my mothers' womb – Psalm 139:13

God guides me everywhere I go – Psalm 139:10
God knows me intimately – Psalm 139:3-4
God prepares my future – Psalm 139:5
God understands me – Psalm 139:6
God keeps every promise He made me – Psalm 138:8
God loves me constantly and endlessly – Jeremiah 31:3
I am God's child – Romans 8:16
God brings everything together good – Romans 8:24
God catches every tear – Psalm 56:8
He delights in me – Psalm 18:19
I am precious in His sight – Isaiah 43:4
God loves me with an everlasting love – Jeremiah 31:3
I have good plans for you – Jeremiah 29:11

Prayer

Help me believe and say the things about myself that God says about me. Amen

Negative words spoken over our lives

The impact of negative words can be brutal. They can limit you and define you. But, as we come into our identity as a child of God these words no longer have any power because, *"the one who is in you is greater than the one who is in the world."* (1 John 4:4) We need to be careful and considerate about our words and the impact they may have. When we are feeling negative about someone, it is important to ask what our Father's narrative on that person's situation is. When we get a divine perspective, it helps us speak the language of love and respond in a way that is honouring of our Father. It is important to ask the question: will our words or actions harm or heal?

Paul's farewell in 2 Corinthians 13:11 AMP says, *"Finally, believers, rejoice! Be made complete [be what you should be], be like-minded, live in peace [enjoy the spiritual well-being experienced by believers who walk closely with God]; and the God of love and peace [the source of lovingkindness] will be with you."* What a wonderful instruction to get right with each other and to receive the blessing of our Father moving amongst us!

We are warned in Galatians 5:13-16 about words that damage our brothers and sisters in Christ. *"You my brothers and sisters were called to be free. But do not use your freedom to indulge the flesh, rather serve one another humbly in love. For the entire law is fulfilled in keeping this one command love you neighbour as yourself. If you bite and devour each other, watch out or you will be destroyed by each other. So, I say, walk by the Spirit, and you will not gratify the desires of the flesh."*

We may come under guilt, condemnation, and shame because we blame ourselves for the things that trigger other people to speak words that harm and hurt. Yet Psalm 49:7 says, *"no one can redeem the life of another or give to God a ransom for them."* They are accountable for what they say or do. Our Father blesses us and does not condemn us. In response to what is said, we may also internalise our own anger and bitterness. This in turn has a consequence on the way we relate to others including Father God. We cannot be accountable for other people's words and actions, but we can consider the words we speak, and have hope. Isaiah 55:3 says, *"give ear and come to me; listen, that you may live."*

As we come to the Father through Jesus and learn how much we are loved and precious to Him, we are brought into truth and healing in Him, knowing that He has a plan and purpose for our life. He will give us strategies to help us in the heat of the fray. Isaiah 30:15 says, *"in repentance and rest is your salvation, in quietness and trust is your strength."* There is nothing we can do or be that will earn the love of the Father. His love is unconditional and cannot be earned. It is freely given.

Negative words we speak into other people's lives or we speak over our own lives

Words we speak to ourselves are immensely powerful and become part of our thought processes. If we constantly say we are fat or ugly or stupid or any other negative thing, we come to believe it, with all the accompanying problems. The power of life and death are in the tongue. When we speak negatively over others, especially if we are in a position of power or authority over them, it is like a curse. They believe what we say and act accordingly. When we speak negative words over others or ourselves, they boomerang back on us. We reap what we sow. When we sow negative words, we harm ourselves and others, which in turn will harm and hurt us, as that will impact the relationship we have with them. When we bless, we are coming up higher. We are speaking from a heavenly perspective, believing in God as we bless those who curse us. We are freed from bitterness, anger, resentment, and we leave that person at the foot of the cross. We are not constrained by actions and words that stop us from being the person God made us to be.

Gossip

When we spread gossip about other people, we do a disservice to them and ourselves. Them, because they cannot defend themselves as they are not present. Ourselves, because this is not right before God. And sometimes because it gets back to the people we are talking about, and it damages our relationship with them. We are warned in Proverbs 16:28 NLT that *"a troublemaker plants seeds of strife; gossip separates the best of friends."*

Complaining and grumbling

If you complain and grumble it means you think that God has got it wrong. This means you are putting your own opinion above God's, and that you think you could do a better job than He does. We all know how ridiculous that is of course! However, people have been complaining and grumbling for hundreds of years. Back in the Old Testament we are told how the Israelites complained and groaned about being freed from the Egyptians and being led through the desert for forty years. However, if they had trusted God, they would have done the journey to the Promised Land so much quicker. You see, complaining and grumbling are a lack of trust in God and His goodness and ability to fulfil what He has promised. It is well worth reading the whole story of the way God rescued the Israelites and gave them a promised land; this can be found in Exodus 1 through to the end of chapter 17. However, we see in Exodus 16:2: *"In the desert the whole community grumbled against Moses and Aaron"*. The interesting thing is they were grumbling about people not just God. Aaron and Moses were God's chosen leaders to save them, and they grumbled even after seeing miraculous ways God worked to save them and seeing God give them miraculous provision. When we complain against leaders or against God then we cannot receive God's blessings.

Criticism

(Lisa) I remember years ago as a young Christian being in a church where I began to get critical of the leadership. There was a moment when the Lord spoke to me through 2 Corinthians 13:10, where it speaks of building up not tearing down. I felt chastened. Quite rightly as I was spreading a negative view and operating out of a spirit of judgement rather than love. 2 Corinthians 13:9-12 says, *"We are glad whenever we are weak but you are strong; and our prayer is that you may be fully restored. This is why I write these things when I am absent, that when I come I may not have to be harsh in my use of authority – the authority the Lord gave me for building you up, not tearing you down. Finally brothers and sisters, rejoice! Strive for full restoration, encourage one another, be of one mind, live in peace. And the God of love and peace will be with you."* When we are freed from a critical attitude, we are able to enjoy others and be constructive rather than destructive in our language.

Judgement

We should never judge anyone, as that is God's prerogative. Only He can give true judgement. David got it right when in 1 Samuel 24:15 he said, *"May the Lord be our judge and decide between us. may he consider my cause and uphold it;*

may he vindicate me by delivering me from your hand."
When we do judge, this gives us wrong attitudes to people or situations and puts a barrier between us and God.

In Matthew 7:3-5 we read, *"Why do you look at the speck of sawdust in your brother's eye and pay no attention to the plank in your own eye? How can you say to your brother, "Let me take the speck out of your eye," when all the time there is a plank in your own eye? You hypocrite, first take the plank out of your own eye, and then you can see clearly to remove the speck from your brother's eye"*

It is alright to have an opinion. We are called to challenge injustice and support others. But an opinion becomes a judgement when our focus becomes personal. Ephesians 6:12 makes clear that, *"our struggle is not against flesh and blood, but against the rulers, against the authorities, against the powers of this dark world and against the spiritual forces of evil in the heavenly realms."*

Accusation

Picture the scene. Jesus is in the temple courts, about to teach those who had gathered around Him and, just at this moment, the Pharisees and the teachers of the law bring to Him a woman who has been caught in adultery. She is made to stand before everyone. They say *"Teacher, this woman was caught in the act of adultery. In the Law Moses commanded us to stone such women. Now what do you say?"* (John 8:4-5). They ask this because they want to trap Him so they can accuse Him. Jesus does not immediately respond, but bends down and begins to write with His finger on the ground. They keep questioning Him. Jesus straightens up and answers. *"All right, but let the one who has never sinned throw the first stone!" Then he stooped down again and wrote in the dust. When the accusers heard this, they slipped away one by one, beginning with the oldest, until only Jesus was left in the middle of the crowd with the woman. Then Jesus stood up again and said to the woman, "Where are your accusers? Didn't even one of them condemn you?" "No, Lord," she said. And Jesus said, "Neither do I. Go and sin no more."* (John 8:7-11 NLT)

It is so easy to accuse others, neglecting our own sin in the process.

A few years ago, I (Lisa) wrote a poem called "The Stone" in response to the story of the woman caught in adultery. I thought of times when I had held something against someone or something, and how in the end the only way to find peace was to drop it. To talk to God about it and give it to Him. To recognise my own need of God to work in my heart in that situation. Sometimes I pick things up after I have let go of them, so I need to drop them again. But, over time God has worked, to His glory. As you read this poem you may like to hold a stone or an object. At the end of the poem, you can drop it to the ground, symbolic of letting go of a judgement against someone else.

The Stone

I held the stone in my hand. Its roughness satisfying, engaging. My eyes focused on the subject of my judgement and indignation. I held the stone in my hand. Its weight distracted me from what was important. My heart filled with a river of fire which could not be contained. I held the stone in my hand, and I looked for others to join me in this cause. My eyes searched for others who were similarly affected and mobilised. I held the stone in my hand and my spirit sank to my feet as I realised, I could not cast the first stone. For as I looked on, I saw the cross, I saw my sin and I knew I had to drop it. I looked to Jesus and asked where would He be in this situation? And I saw mercy not judgement, grace not indignation, love not hatred. And the cause was surrendered to Him who is able to accomplish more than we could ask or imagine.

Bearing grudges

It is so easy to hold something against someone. Leviticus 19:18 says, *"Do not seek revenge or bear a grudge against anyone among your people, but love your neighbour as yourself. I am the Lord."* It is important to be attentive to what is in our hearts. Proverbs 4:23 NASB says. *"watch over your heart with all diligence, for from it flow the springs of life."*

Bitterness

(Lisa) At crossroad moments I have often been reminded of some wise words in an email I once received, "you have the choice between being bitter or better." I have often prayed to Father God asking for help not to be bitter. Sometimes I have been able by God's grace to do this. Other times it has been much harder. It has been like an onion where I have had layer and layer of emotion to work through to slowly bring a shift and a breakthrough. I have found there is a peace that passes all understanding as I surrender my bitterness to my loving Father.

We may live in a situation where someone else close to us is bitter. We are not responsible for their choices to do this. Our Father knows what has happened and what they are going through. As we look to our Father, He will lead us and guide us as to what to do and say and how to pray.

Hebrews 12:15 says *"See to it that no one falls short of the grace of God and that no bitter root grows up to cause trouble and define many."* Bitterness causes trouble and can destroy relationships both with God and others.

Grievance

We may be unhappy about something. I remember hearing a story in 2006 about Timberline church in America. How Nicky the stripper came to faith and then others she knew also came to faith. They came to Timberline church with their children. Their behaviour and language were different from the established church goers. There was a moment when the church leader was approached by a lady in the congregation. She said to him "you have ruined our church". Dary Northrop, the Senior Pastor at Timberline Church at the time, who did not know what to do, simply said "yes I know". They talked together for a while and this lady changed her attitude. When asked what the church should do? Her answer was "I guess we'll have to love them". God had worked in her heart. Be open to the Holy Spirit, shifting your perspective about something and helping you bless others.

Fear

Fear is one of the most frequent human emotions. In fact, the Bible tells us 365 times do not be afraid. Coincidence? I do not think so. I believe God knows every day we would have a choice to be afraid or live in faith. Faith and fear cannot coexist. Whatever we are afraid of, we are making bigger than God. This is saying God's blessings will not make a significant change in our life and situation, and prevents us from seeing the possible blessings, let alone receiving them. Fear is a lack of faith in God, and we are told in Hebrews 11:6 *"without faith it is impossible to please God, because anyone who comes to him must believe that he exists and that he rewards those who earnestly seek him"*.

Therefore, we must not be fearful but instead have faith so we can receive God's blessings. However, if you do have fear in your life you can repent and ask God to fill you with His perfect love which casts out fear, then you can be in faith that God wants to and will bless you, and you can receive His blessings and thank Him for them.

Fear of man

If you bow to human opinion, you are not listening to or taking notice of God's opinion. You cannot serve God and man. If you are constantly worried about what people might say and think then you are not putting God's opinion and desires first. You have to make a choice. Whose opinion is most important God's or man's? Who will you please? God or man? Fear of man is the root of appeasement. God has given us the emotion of fear to protect and warn us, so we still need His wisdom in each situation.

Appeasement

Appeasement means to make concessions to someone, such as an aggressor or a critic, often at the sacrifice of principles. We can appease others to keep the peace or out of fear of getting hurt in some way. The one who appeases sees themselves as the weakest in the situation and has low self-worth and self-esteem. Appeasement is giving people what they want to prevent them harming or being angry with you. This can stop you from receiving God's blessing, as you are more aware of what people can do for you than God.

Jealousy

If you are jealous of someone it means you feel God is not treating you fairly or is treating someone else better than you. You are not content with what God has given you and you are not thankful. This puts a block between you and God. The truth is God loves each person as much, but shows that love in ways suited to each person. He loves each one of us as much as He loves His son Jesus, but He shows He loves us in different ways. As parents we love our children as much as each other but we show it in different ways according to their personalities and how they receive love. I (Wendy) have four boys and two love hugs, whilst the other two would rather not have hugs as much. So, I hug the two that love hugs more than I do the other two (though I still hug them), but I show the other two love in the way that they prefer. God knows what we need and gives that to us. The truth is, there will always be people better off than you and there will always be people worse off than you, so you need to be thankful for what you have. If you do not compare your life with others, you will not be jealous and will be more content. Instead of looking at other people and what they have, look at your own life and what you have and be grateful for your life.

Anger

Anger is not always wrong. We may feel anger about an injustice. It is what we do with anger in our thoughts and actions that can make it a sin. In Ephesians 4:26-29 we are instructed, *"In your anger do not sin: Do not let the sun go down while you are still angry, and do not give the devil a foothold."* Jesus says in Matthew 5:22, *"But I tell you that anyone who is angry with a brother or sister will be subject to judgement."* Jesus taught *"if you are offering your gift at the altar and there remember that your brother or sister has something against you, leave your gift there in front of the altar. First go and be reconciled to them; then come and offer your gift."* (Matthew 5:23-24)

We are told anger is a sin, and as soon as we realise we are angry we need to ask God to forgive us and help us to deal with our anger. We can be angry at others, at ourselves and at God. If we are angry at someone, it means we have judged them and think they have done something wrong, so we will need to forgive them. We also need to ask God for forgiveness for judging people, ourselves, or God. We have no right to judge anyone. If we are angry at ourself, it means we have judged ourself and that is God's job not ours. It may well mean that we have not accepted God's forgiveness even when we have said sorry for what we have done or said. This is putting ourself and our opinion above God's. It is obvious if we are angry at God, we are in the wrong! God does not do things worth us being angry at Him. We misunderstand situations and think God has caused them or could have stopped them. For instance, if someone kills you or someone you love with no reason, you may blame God and be angry that He did not stop them. However, God gives EVERYONE free will, so He could not have stopped them without overriding their free will. We all want to have free will ourselves, but do not like someone else having free will when they choose to do something we don't agree with. If we are angry with God, we need to say sorry and admit to Him we were wrong; God will forgive us, things will be right again and there is no hindrance to being blessed after that.

Lack of self control

If you had a recording of what you were speaking, what sort of things would you hear played back? In James 3:6 NLT, we are warned that *"among all the parts of the body, the tongue is a flame of fire. It is a whole world of wickedness, corrupting your entire body. It can set your whole life on fire, for it is set on fire by hell itself."* We need to be alert and vigilant about how the tongue can be destructive if we do not exercise self-control and discernment from a place of integrity and truth. In James 3:9 we read how the tongue can be used for good or for evil. James says, *"with the tongue we praise our Lord and Father, and with it we curse human beings, who have been made in God's likeness. Out of the same mouth come praise and cursing. My brothers this should not be. Can both fresh water and saltwater flow from the same spring? My brothers can a fig tree bear olives, or a grapevine bear figs? Neither can a salt spring produce fresh water."*

Sin

God is holy and for us to be in relationship with Him we need to be right with Him. This means saying sorry for our failures and sins as soon as we recognise them and asking for His forgiveness. He always forgives us when we ask. Sin puts a hindrance and a barrier between us and God but as soon as we repent, God forgives us, and all barriers are removed.

Psalm 103:11-13 NRSV says, *"For as the heavens are high above the earth, so great is his steadfast love toward those who fear him; as far as the east is from the west, so far he removes our transgressions from us. As a father has compassion for his children, so the Lord has compassion for those who fear him."* Isn't this amazing? Stop for a moment and think what this means for you. His steadfast love is there to bring you close to Him. His love for you is as far as the east is from the west. Think of a sea horizon that goes on and on, and you get a glimpse of how vast God's love is. What is more, this is how far He removes our sins from us. God has compassion for you. He longs for the best for you. This is the good news. Spend some time now and see if there is anything God shows you that stands in the way between you both.

Disobedience

Jonah had a message from God. Words that would lead to Nineveh repenting and getting right with God. Yet what did Jonah do? He went on the run onto a ship. In the storm he was below decks not helping the sailors. When challenged, he said what he was doing, and he was thrown into the sea where he was swallowed by a whale. He then prayed to God and was spewed up on land where he did what God had asked him to do. When Nineveh repented, in response Jonah, instead of praising God, got angry. God then helped him understand His love and concern for every person of Nineveh. If Jonah had not ultimately been obedient sharing the message God had given him, the blessing of repentance and transformation would have been withheld. The good news is that when we do disobey a prompting of the Holy Spirit, we can be honest about this with our Father, asking for His forgiveness. Father God, time and time again, gives us opportunities to share His love and care with others, as we are obedient to the leading of the Holy Spirit.

Lack of unity

We are warned not to be divided. In Galatians 5:20-21 it warns us against *".... hatred, discord, jealousy, fits of rage, selfish ambition, dissensions, factions.... Those who live like this will not inherit the kingdom of God."* God's blessing is with those who live together in unity. This does not mean we have to agree about everything, but we are united in our belief and trust in Christ. We serve side by side as we have opportunity for God's kingdom purposes.

Using freedom wisely

Our Father's heart is that we will be blessed with freedom from fear and every other bondage that would seek to hurt or harm us. But we are cautioned not to use our freedoms to indulge in the flesh, rather to serve one another humbly in love *"for the entire law is fulfilled in keeping this one command. Love your neighbour as yourself. If you bite and devour each other, watch out or you will be destroyed by each other. So, I say walk by the spirit and you will not gratify the desires of the flesh."* (Galatians 5:14-16)

Weakness

It is so easy to find ourselves overwhelmed by our own frailties. Yet Father God delights to work in our weakness to His glory. Paul three times pleaded for the Lord to take away the thorn in his side. Then God spoke to him and said *"my grace is all you need. My power works best in weakness."* (2 Corinthians 12:9) Paul changed his direction of thinking in the second half of this verse, in his response when he says, *"So now I am glad to boast about my weaknesses, so that the power of Christ can work through me."* We do not give up, but give up to our Father all that we have lost hope in, all that is raw and sore, and Father God comforts us and brings His healing and revelation. He helps us face each day, each situation. He gives us life giving words, life changing words. Words that build up not tear down. Words that bring people together as part of an expression of God's love and care.

Weariness

It is hard to bless when we are weary. Galatians 6:9-10 says, *"So let's not get tired of doing what is good. At just the right time we will reap a harvest of blessing if we don't give up. Therefore, whenever we have the opportunity, we should do good to everyone – especially to those in the family of faith."* It is so important that we rest. To have our sabbath rest. In Isaiah 30:15 TLB it says, *"Only in returning to me and waiting for me will you be saved; in quietness and*

confidence is your strength; but you'll have none of this."
Help us Father to rest. Bring your healing and restoration as we do. Amen

Isolation

Sometimes we may find ourselves isolated and lonely. Isolation causes us to be removed from other people's lives whether physically, emotionally, or spiritually. It may be for all sorts of reasons. We may have memories, regrets and pain that make it hard to be with others. Yet our Father is near. He is there with us. He does not leave us without a comforter. He catches every tear. Psalm 56:8 says *"You keep track of all my sorrows. You have collected all my tears in your bottle. You have recorded each one in your book."* As we spend time with Him, we are not alone. He can minister into our hearts and lives. We can receive His blessing and from that overflow, bless others as the Holy Spirit leads us. Deuteronomy 31:8 ESV says, *"It is the Lord who goes before you. He will be with you; he will not leave you or forsake you. Do not fear or be dismayed."*

Not tithing

Malachi 3:10 shows the importance of tithing and how it is connected to being blessed by God. It says *"Bring the whole tithe into the storehouse, that there may be food in my house. Test me in this,"* says the Lord Almighty, *"and see if I will not throw open the floodgates of heaven and pour out so much blessing that there will not be room enough to store it."* There are many more places in the Bible that say similar.

Not following God's commands

When we follow God's commandments, He blesses us. When we don't, it is hard to receive His blessing.

Things that entice and tempt

Words can be traps and snares. Not everyone is looking out for our good. We live in a fallen world. We need to be vigilant and prayerful so we can enjoy all the blessings God has for us.

Our thought life

A few years ago, I watched the film "What women want". The main male character could hear what women were thinking in their minds. I know if my thoughts were spoken out loud, they would not always be honouring of God. 2 Corinthians 10:5 encourages us to, *"take captive every thought to make it obedient to Christ."* Philippians 4:8 says *"...whatever is noble, whatever is right, whatever is pure, whatever is lovely, whatever is admirable – if anything is excellent or praiseworthy – think about such things."* What we feed our minds will influence our language.

Conclusions

These are some of the ways we can stop ourselves from receiving God's blessings. Most of these things will be because we have wrong attitudes and do not carry God's heart for people. Unless we come into agreement with the way God sees things or people, we will not be able to bless them with God's Father's blessing.

Some of the obstacles to being blessed ourselves will also be obstacles to blessing others. These include anger, unforgiveness, judgement, grumbling, fear, sin, and jealousy. Other obstacles are bitterness, offense, and rebellion. Any thought or reaction not in agreement with God's way will mean it is hard for you to bless others, as your heart attitude will be wrong. You need to bless people from a heart of love, from seeing them as God sees them and with His love.

The last thing is we can curse people by what we say. We might not mean to curse them, but when we say negative things to people or about people and situations and places, we are cursing them. For example, if you say to someone they are stupid, over time they will believe it and start acting that way.

Language is powerful and language creates reality. We need to be careful what we say and how we say it. This hit me afresh when I saw an interview on a mum who has a baby who has Down's Syndrome, and she has made language cards on how to talk about people who have Down's Syndrome or parents of children who have it. This was on the BBC, and you can watch it if you wish by checking on Google.

Ask God if there is anything that is a barrier either to you receiving His blessing for yourself or to you blessing others; then listen, and when He tells you something deal with it with him through prayer.

Going deeper

- Think of the things you are thankful for and all the blessings in your life. Spend time thanking God for these.
  Here are some examples to start you off.... A sunrise, a sunset, a walk, food, shelter, company, and interests....
- Spend time reading through the 10 commandments in Exodus 20:1-17. Have an honest conversation with God about any commandments you struggle with and ask for His help.

Questions

- What do you consider to be a spiritual blessing?
- What do you think some of the obstacles to receiving blessing are?
- Can you recognise the blessings that God gives you? If you do, are you grateful for them? Write down some of the things that come to mind.
- Do you find it easy to listen? What stops you from listening?
- Is what God says about you what you say about yourself? If not, where you differ in what you say?

Start saying the thing God says to counteract the things you say.

Letter

My dear child,

Let me show you things that put a distance between us and stop you from fully receiving all my blessings. I love you and long to bless you in all areas of your life, so anything that stops you receiving my blessing is a great sadness to me. I know you want to be close to me and receive my blessings so let's talk about these things as Father and child. Soon you will be walking in the fullness of my blessing. You will be amazed at the difference this makes to your life.

Love, your Dad, Almighty God

Prayer

Heavenly Father

Please help me be aware of anything that would stop me walking in the fullness of your blessing. I am sorry for (name specific things as God shows you) that would stop me from walking in your Father's blessing.

Amen

Blessing

Be blessed to have every obstacle removed so that you can receive the Father's blessing freely.

Songs

So freely by Dave Bilborough (1997)
Count your Blessings by Guy Penrod (2012)
You say by Lauren Daigle (2018)

Optional extra reading

Under Cover: The promise of Protection Under His Authority: The Key to Living in God's Provision and Proection by John Bevere (2012)
Bait of satan by John Bevere (2014)
The devil's door by John Bevere (1996)

Chapter 4

Blessings in the prodigal son

Most people know the parable of the prodigal son really well and there have been many insights as to what Jesus was revealing through the parable, but I (Wendy) believe God has given me a new revelation about what God is like as Father and how He loves to bless His children through this parable. The parable can be found in Luke 15:11-32. The parable is really showing that the Father in the parable is like our heavenly Father. It is also showing the many ways the Father in the parable poured blessings on both of his sons, just like our Heavenly Father does with us.

What struck us as we have been looking again at the prodigal son is that we were drawn to focus on the loving father.

The lost son

Jesus went on to say, "There was once a man who had two sons. The younger one said to him, 'Father, give me my share of the property now.' So the man divided his property between his two sons. After a few days the younger son sold his part of the property and left home with the money. He went to a country far away, where he wasted his money in reckless living. He spent everything he had. Then a severe famine spread over that country, and he was left without a thing. So he went to work for one of the citizens of that country, who sent him out to his farm to take care of the pigs. He wished he could fill himself with the bean pods the pigs ate, but no one gave him anything to eat. At last he came to his senses and said, 'All my father's hired workers have more than they can eat, and here I am about to starve I will get up and go to my father and say, "Father, I have sinned against God and against you. I am no longer fit to be called your son; treat me as one of your hired workers."' So he got up and started back to his father.

"He was still a long way from home when his father saw him; his heart was filled with pity, and he ran, threw his arms around his son, and kissed him. "Father" the son said, "I have sinned against God and against you. I am no longer fit to be called your son." But the father called to his servants. "Hurry!" he said. "Bring the best robe and put it on him. Put a ring on his finger and shoes on his feet. Then go and get the prize calf and kill it, and let us celebrate with a feast! For this son of mine was dead, but now he is alive; he was lost, but now he has been found." And so the feasting began.

"In the meantime the older son was out in the field. On his way back, when he came close to the house, he heard the music and dancing So he called one of the servants and asked him, "What's going on?" "Your brother has come back home," the servant answered, "and your father has killed the prize calf, because he got him back safe and sound." The older brother was so angry that he would not go into the house; so his father came out and begged him to come in. But he spoke back to his father, "Look, all these years I have worked for you like a slave, and I have never disobeyed your orders. What have you given me? Not even a goat for me to have a feast with my friends! But this son of yours wasted all your property on prostitutes, and when he comes back home, you kill the prize calf for him!" "My son," the father answered, "you are always here with me, and everything I have is yours. But we had to celebrate and be happy, because your brother was dead, but now he is alive; he was lost, but now he has been found."" (Luke 15:11-32 GNT)

When we look at this version of the story of the prodigal, the title is "the lost son". Some people believe that it should be called the parable of the lost sons. As we were writing, we felt the focus of what we should write about was the loving father. This is what we are going to look at in this chapter.

The importance of the relationship of love between the father in the parable and his sons is shown by the way he is introduced as *"There was once a man who had two sons."* (Luke 15:11 GNT) Both the father and the sons are known by their relationship with each other. Our Heavenly Father also holds us in great love as we are told in Psalm 139:16 GNT: *"you saw me before I was born. The days allotted to me had all been recorded in your book, before any of them ever began."* This shows how much the Father loves His children and how well He knows them and plans for them. This is the blessing of having parents who love and plan for you. As was said, the father in the story shows what our Heavenly Father is like. Our Heavenly Father loves and knows us and has good plans for us.

This father is constantly blessing his sons. The story starts with the sons already being adults and living with their father, helping run the farm (the family business). We have to assume that the father has loved and provided for them all through their childhood, which is yet another blessing. This is the blessing of being loved and provided for. Our Heavenly Father has always loved and provided for us, and always will. Jeremiah 31:3 says, *"I have loved you with an everlasting love."* Also, in Genesis 22:14, we are told that the Lord will provide.

The sons and father working together and living together on the family farm is also the blessing of being included and working together towards a common goal, and the blessing of spending time together. Time spent together focused on a common cause helps with communication and is a sign of love. It is said love is spelt TIME. God asks us to focus on His kingdom and that we live in His Kingdom. He is always present with us. In Hebrews 13:5, God has said, *"Never will I leave you; never will I forsake you."* In the Lord's Prayer we are told to pray *"your kingdom come, your will be done, on earth as it is in heaven."* (Matthew 6:10)

There is also the blessing of having an inheritance. This father has made an inheritance for his sons. God gives us an inheritance too. Colossians 3:24 says, *"since you know that you will receive an inheritance from the Lord as a reward."*

The next blessings are the blessing of mercy and generosity. When the youngest son asks for his inheritance while the father is alive it was a great insult, virtually saying I wish you were dead, or your money means more than our relationship. The father would have had every right to throw him off the property and disinherit him, and indeed this would have been the way people would have expected the father to react. However, the father in the parable shows the blessings of mercy and generosity by giving the youngest son his inheritance and, not only that, he gives the blessing of generosity by giving the eldest son his inheritance also. God also gives us mercy as in Psalm 23 NKJV it says, *"Surely goodness and mercy will follow me; all the days of my life."* Jesus says in John 10:10 *"I have come that they may have life, and have it to the full."* This is the blessing of generosity.

Another blessing is having the blessing of a father who has no favourites. Both sons were treated equally and given their share of the inheritance at the same time. God also has no favourites. Colossians 3:25 says *"there is no favouritism."*

Giving the sons their inheritance early shows the blessing of the sons being put before the father's needs, as by giving them their inheritance before he has died it obviously means the father's income is reduced. Father God is like that with us, as He gives us our inheritance while we are alive and can use it, and at a cost to himself as He gave up His son Jesus to save us. This also shows us the blessing of mercy and unconditional love and generosity.

Included in the act of giving the sons their inheritance is the blessing of freedom of choice. The father put no conditions or restrictions on how they spent their inheritance. He even gave them the blessing of wasting their inheritance if that was their choice. God the Father always gives us the blessing of freedom of choice. He even gives us the choice to walk away from Him just as the younger son did with the father in the parable. Galatians 5:1 says, *"It is for freedom that Christ has set us free."*

Also included by giving them their inheritance is the blessing of provision, and Father God also gives us this as a blessing. Philippians 4:19 ESV, *"And my God will supply every need of yours according to his riches in glory in Christ Jesus."*

Luke 15:20 GNT says *"...So he got up and started back to his father. "He was still a long way from home when his father saw him; his heart was filled with pity, and he ran, threw his arms around his son, and kissed him."* This shows the father must have been constantly looking for the son to have seen him from a long distance. Father God is always watching for us, and Psalm 139 tells us this is because He is thinking about us all the time. It is a blessing to have parents that constantly long for you and look for you. This is a blessing of being wanted and loved. This shows your importance to your parents and is a sign of love.

This verse also says the father ran to meet him while he was a long way off. This is the blessing of protection. In those days, the village chiefs would have been insulted by the way the son had treated his father, as it was a lack of respect for the elders and tradition and wasn't showing honour. This was very important to them, and they would have been worried other children would copy the sons' behaviour. They had the right to turn him away from the village and to say to never return or even to kill him. However, if the father got there first and accepted him back, they could not do anything against the son. The father wanted to get there first and protect his son.

This verse also shows the blessing of having a wise father. The father's wisdom was shown by him looking out for his son and running to him to protect him from the anger of the villagers.

The last blessing in this verse is the blessing of having a father who is aware of other people's feelings and who is a peacemaker and well respected. This is shown by the way the villagers don't attack the son and come to the party for him. This shows respect for the father and that he is well liked.

The father's blessing included the gift of complete forgiveness and restoration. As soon as the youngest son returned, he was giving the blessing of a wonderful welcome, forgiven and restored to a place in the family immediately. This is also the blessing of unconditional love. God forgives and restores us when we return to Him and invite Jesus into our lives. We too have a wonderful welcome home. Luke 15:7 says, *"I tell you in the same way there will be more rejoicing in Heaven over one sinner who repents than over ninety-nine righteous persons who do not need to repent.*

Forgiveness included the blessing of covering shame. The father put his own cloak on the son to cover him and his poor attire. Father God gives us the gift of righteousness and we are covered in Jesus' righteousness. 1 Corinthians 1:30, *"It is because of him that you are in Christ Jesus who has become for us wisdom from |God"* - that is our righteousness, holiness, and redemption. This covers all our shame. Also Psalm 3:3 TLB says, *"But Lord, you are my shield, my glory, and my only hope. You alone can lift my head, now bowed in shame."*

The forgiveness gave the prodigal the blessing of a clean start and starting afresh as if nothing had ever gone wrong. Father God does this by forgiving our sins if we ask Jesus into our hearts.

The blessing of acceptance as was given by the father as he hugged the son and ran to meet him before he apologised or washed or changed anything. Dressed like a beggar and smelling of the pigsty the father welcomed him home wholeheartedly. Father God does this, as we are told in Romans 5:8 *"But God demonstrates his own love for us in this: While we were still sinners Christ died for us."*

The blessing shown by the giving of the ring was the blessing of acting with the father's authority, and therefore the blessing of being trusted is included. This is the father giving the blessing of faith in the son and seeing the good in him that he could not even see in himself. It is telling him he is trustworthy. Father God also gives us the blessing of acting with the Father's authority and being trusted by Him. Luke 10:19 says, *"I have given you authority to trample on snakes and scorpions and to overcome all the power of the enemy; nothing will harm you."*

The blessing shown by the giving of the sandals is the blessing of being not only returned to full sonship but being known as a son. It was an outward sign of sonship and belonging to a family, as only sons and daughters wore shoes; other people who were slaves or servants did not wear shoes. Father God also gives us outward signs of sonship by giving us shoes of peace as part of our spiritual armour, as we are told in Ephesians 6:15 NLT, *"For shoes, put on the peace that comes from the Good News so that you will be fully prepared."*

The father throwing a feast is the blessing of having a father who is proud of you and celebrates you in front of other people. Father God did this with Jesus at His baptism. In Matthew 3:17, as Jesus comes up out of the water His Father says, *"This is my son, whom I love; with him I am well pleased."* We are told that Father God loves us as much as Jesus, so He does the same for us. Also, in Isaiah 43, God talks of how much He loves His people and verse 4 says, *"since you are precious and honoured in my sight, and because I love you, I will give people in exchange for you."* This also gives the blessing of self-esteem and self-worth.

However, the father in the parable not only blesses the younger son but also the elder son. They both have shared equal blessings whilst living with their father, but also the elder son is given the blessing of provision and generosity by receiving his share of the inheritance whilst the father is still alive.

Not only does he get his inheritance but, because he is living at home, he has access to all that the father has. We too have access to all that Father God has. Romans 8:32 AMP says, *"He who did not spare [even]His own Son, but gave Him up for us all, how will He not also, along with Him, graciously give us all things?"* The elder son shares the same blessing of inclusion into the family and sharing in the celebration, as the father goes to bring the eldest son into the party.

It may help to have a list of all the blessings that are included in the Father's blessing, both from the father in the parable and that Father God also blesses us with:

The blessing of...

...a Father who loves us.
...a Father who is generous.
...a Father who spends time with us.
...a Father who works on things together with us.
...a Father who gives us a joint focus.
...a Father who plans for us.
...a Father who gives us an inheritance.
...a Father who constantly blesses us.
...a Father who doesn't have favourites.
...mercy.
...forgiveness.
...unconditional love.
...being put ahead of the Father's needs.
...provision.
...being wanted and cared for by your Father.
...restoration and complete inclusion in the family after
...wrongdoing.
...protection.
...freedom of choice.
...a wise Father.
...a Father who is aware of other's feelings and is respected.
...a Father who covers our shame.
...no restrictions.
...being trusted.
...being given authority.
...being given responsibilities.
...belonging.
...being accepted just as you are.
...your Father seeing the best in you.

...your Father being proud of you and acknowledging you in front of everyone.

...access to all your Father has.

...self-esteem and self-worth.

...the outward signs of sonship.

...being known as your Father's child.

...identity.

...being celebrated.

...being part of a family.

All these blessings show that the Father's blessing and the Father's love are inextricably linked together. You cannot know the Father's love without knowing the Father's blessing, and you cannot know the Father's blessing without knowing the Father's love. You cannot know either without knowing the Father's heart. THE FATHER'S BLESSING DEMONSTRATES THE FATHER'S LOVE.

The sons in the story could not see their father's love or blessings and did not receive them, and the reason for this was they did not know their father's heart. How do we know this? If the younger son had known his father's heart he would have never asked for his inheritance, and the elder brother would have prevented him from doing so. They would have known that they had access to everything their father had anyway. When the younger son came on hard times he would have returned home immediately before things got so bad, because he would have known his father would welcome him home. Also, when he did go home, he would have known his father would welcome him back and would restore him to full sonship, he would not have thought he would have to ask to become a servant.

The elder son would not have waited for the prodigal to come home but would have gone and fetched him back, as he would have known how heartbroken his father was. Also, he wouldn't have been jealous of his brother's welcome home and the love shown to him, because he would have been secure in his father's love and known that he would be treated the same. He would not have felt like a slave rather than a son and would have known he could have anything his father had without his father spelling it out. He would have gone into the party because he would have known how important his presence was to his father. Neither son felt like a son or acted like a son. They didn't know their father's heart or how loved and blessed they were.

Do you know God the Father's heart? Do you know and see the blessings He gives you? Do you receive His blessings? Do you know God the Father's love?

If we look at the definition of love in 1 Corinthians 13, we can see how all the Father's' blessings are present in the description of love. We shouldn't be surprised at this as we are told that God the Father is love in 1 John 4:8. God is love. 1 Corinthians 13:4-8 says, *"Love is patient, love is kind, it does not envy, it does not boast, it is not proud. It does not dishonour others, it is not self-seeking, it is not easily angered, it keeps no record of wrongs. Love does not delight in evil but rejoices with the truth. It always protects, always hopes, always perseveres. Love never fails."*

The father patiently waited for his son to come home. This is love is patient. Love is kind is shown in the way the father handled his sons request for his inheritance. Love does not envy is shown by the way the father did not begrudge his son having a good time with his inheritance. Love does not dishonour others it is not self-seeking is the way the father put his own needs aside to let the children have their inheritance early and did not think of his own needs. It is not easily angered is shown by the way he reacted to his son asking for his inheritance and the elder son refusing to come into the party. It keeps no record of wrongs is shown by the father immediately welcoming his child back as a son. It does not delight in evil but rejoices with the truth is shown by the way the father reacts in love with both sons and does not rehash all they have done wrong. The father in the story protected his son from the anger that the other villagers would have had toward the son. The father looking out for his son coming home shows that he was always hoping and always persevering. Love never fails is shown by the way the father kept loving both sons regardless of their behaviour. Truly the father in the prodigal son shows how loving God is as our Father and how He is a Father who loves to bless. In all His ways, like the father in the parable, God is a Father who always loves and always blesses His children. What a blessing to have a Father like that!

Below is a word Lisa received from God.

As my spirit works in hearts and lives, my grace will transform and renew, challenge and call. I do not look on the outside, but I look at the heart of my people. I have heard the prayers of my people and I will not tarry. Look onto the horizon and see there are people journeying back to me and, like the loving father I am running to them to embrace them. To acknowledge each person as a precious child of mine without judgement but celebrating their return.

The Father heart of God

(Lisa) I remember the moment. I had just taken communion at my church and was sat in quiet reflection. Suddenly I had the words "prodigal watch, watch the prodigals". It was an instruction. I did not know what it meant. Only when I read through the parable of the lost son did it make sense. I understood for the first time how the father was longing for his son to return home. Watching for any movement back to him. Running to him when he did. Embracing him. Celebrating his return. The same is true when we return to God. Yet, there was also another son who stayed at home who did not want to join in with the celebration when his brother returned. He was bitter that his brother was being welcomed after all he had done. He missed the amazing, extravagant, forgiving, wonderful love of the father.

In our families, on our streets and in our communities, there will be people who have in the past had a relationship with God. Some may have gone off and done their own thing. Others may have become disillusioned with church and left. There are also people who have faithfully stayed with church who struggle with the Father's love for those who return. They are indignant that they can come back and become part of the family of God again. Their focus is on what that person has done, not on what God is doing. So, when we think about prodigals returning, what are they returning to? Are they returning to the Father's House? So, what is the Father's House?

My Father's House, as Jesus taught about it, was the temple and that was where the priest proclaimed the blessing. The Father's house is more to do with the atmosphere and being full of God's presence than the building. God's house would be full of the fruit of the Holy Spirit. The Father's house takes on the character and values of the parents. God our Heavenly Father wants us to return home to Him. He wants us to live our lives with the Father's house as our security, our firm foundation, our base, so that we daily go out into the world we always return home at night to the Father's house. God the Father's house would be welcoming, full of love, plenty of provision, where you get fed, where you learn. If you do not know your Father's heart you will not understand the culture of the Father's house. Galatians 5:22-23 AMP says, *"the fruit of the Spirit [the result of His presence within us] is love [unselfish concern for others], joy, [inner] peace, patience [not the ability to wait, but how we act while waiting], kindness, goodness, faithfulness, gentleness, self-control...."*. This is the atmosphere that will be in the Father's house. What foundation are you building on? Your Father's house is meant to be the foundation for your life, the springboard that launches you into your future. Words spoken over you in your Father's house can have an effect on you for the rest of your life if you let them. This can be good or bad. We are told in Proverbs 18:21 AMPC, *"Death and life are in the power of the tongue and they who indulge in it shall eat the fruit in it"* (for death or life).

So how do we bless those who return and those who stay? We bless acknowledging that both have the same Father. A Father who loves them. We bless by our encouragement. We are interested in what they are doing and cheer them on. We bless by not keeping people in their past but letting new chapters be written as they respond to God's love and care for them in relationship with others. We bless the new thing but remain vigilant over any places of weakness that may hurt them or others. We bless by hearing people's stories and learning from them, rather than judging them. We bless by recognising how precious they are. How unique they are. We bless them by accepting them as part of the family of God. By celebrating who they are. We bless by journeying with people who have questions and pain. We bless them by practical care and support if necessary. We bless by giving them opportunities to use their giftings and serve in the church. We bless because we know we all fall short. We bless because we have experienced the blessing of the Father's love and we want to do likewise to others. We bless by being willing to go where neither we nor they have been before, as Father God works in our lives.

Take a moment. Ask yourself these questions. As you do, pray in response, asking God to lead you and guide you giving you opportunities to get to know others and to be a blessing to them.

- How many friends do you have who are not Christian?
- How many sports activities and hobbies do you have outside of church?
- What are your passions?
- What do you commit your time to?
- How many people do you connect with in your community who don't go to church?
- Do you know your neighbours?
- Are you waiting for people to come back to church or are you active in reaching out to people where they are?

Perhaps you are a grandparent, parent or sibling and someone in your family no longer believes and/or goes to church. It is so easy to feel you have failed and come under condemnation. Our Father longs for us to give this to Him. To minister into any hurt, pain, and regret.

One of the prophesies I love is, "when the father's house is filled with the father's love, the prodigals will return home". As the world knows we are Christ's disciples because of the way we love each other, this will be a witness and it will be this love that will draw people back into relationship with the Father and other Christians.

The father's house in the parable of the prodigal son

When the elder son returns back home, he returns to the father's house. He returns home to live in his father's house and receive all the blessings the father had for him. If we look, the prodigal son doesn't say he will return to his father and renew the father/child relationship, he says he will return home as even the workers had a better lifestyle than he had. They were provided for and cared for and had enough food to eat. The prodigal actually states, "they lack nothing". This would also assume they were provided with shelter, and in fact they may not have been living in the father's house but almost certainly on the land.

In the same way that the father in the story is meant to show what God is like as our Father, so the father's house in the story is meant to show what God the Father's house is like. So, what is the father's house in the story like?

The father's house in the story must be a wonderful place, as it is this that drew the prodigal son home. He tells how it is a caring place, as all the workers are well looked after and lack nothing. It is a large place, as it accommodates the workers as well as the family. It is a place of fun and laughter and parties, as the father throws a party for everyone to celebrate the son coming home. It is an inclusive place, as the father wants the eldest son as well as the youngest son at the party. The father had invited all the villagers. They all turned up, so it must be a welcoming place where people can enjoy themselves. In fact, it is a place of great joy as we are told everyone celebrated with overflowing joy. The house represents the father. It is a place of provision.

Most importantly THE FATHERS HOUSE IS A HOUSE OF BLESSING. We have previously listed all the blessings the father gave his sons within his house, and the father's house has its atmosphere or culture defined by the character of the father.

Going deeper

How can you get to know God the Father's heart more?

Talk to God the Father and ask Him to draw you closer to Him. Ask Him to help you know His love and blessing at a heart level.

Spend time just being with God and listen to what He has to say to you.

Questions

- Is there one thing that stood out for you in the parable of the prodigal son?
- Do you identify with the young son or the elder brother?

Letter

My dear child,

That is what you are, even though you walked away from me. You will always be my child and I will always love you. I watch out for you every day, waiting for a sign of you coming home. As soon as I see that, I will run to meet you and gather you in my arms surrounding you with my love. There is nothing you can do or say or think that will stop my love for you. I am your Father and I love you with an unconditional love. I can't wait to welcome you home and live in a father/child relationship with you again. Everything I have is yours and with everything within me I love you. You are part of me, and I am constantly thinking of you and looking out for you. I know everything about you, and I am calling out to you to come home. Everything you need can be found in me and I give you every good thing. I bless you with everything you need and fulfil your desire for good things. Come back home and live life in abundance.

Love, Your Dad, Almighty God

Prayer

Heavenly Father I do not want to be a prodigal. Someone who wanders far from you. I want to know your Father's heart for me and live secure in your love and blessing. Thank you that you are the perfect Father and I can enjoy being your child. Please help me to extend the same love and grace you have shown me to others who need to come back to you. Amen

Blessing for prodigals

Be blessed...

> ...to know your heavenly Father loves you.
> ...to know Father God longs for your return.
> ...to know God as your heavenly Father.
> ...to know Father God constantly looks out for you.
> ...to know how precious you are to God.
> ...to come to the end of yourself.
> ...to hit rock bottom.
> ...to come to your senses.
> ...to remember how good your Father is.
> ...to remember life in your Father's house.
> ...to remember how kind and caring your Father is.
> ...to repent.
> ...to return home.
> ...to receive the Father's embrace.
> ...by your heavenly Father's forgiveness.
> ...by your heavenly Father's acceptance of you.
> ...to be welcomed home.
> ...to be treated like a son or daughter.
> ...to have your identity affirmed.
> ...to be part of God's family.

...by your heavenly Father trusting you.

...by having your heavenly Father's authority.

...by being celebrated.

...to with a sense of purpose.

...to be provided for by God.

...with new beginnings.

...to start over with hope.

Songs

No longer slaves by Melissa Helser and Jonathan David Helser (2015)

Prodigal song by Cory Ashbury (2020)

He ran to me (the Prodigal Son) by Phillips, Craig and Dean (1999)

Welcome home by John Nuttal (2007)

Books

Spiritual slavery to spiritual sonship by Jack Frost. (2013)

Sonship - a journey into the Father's heart by James Jordan (2014)

The road home by J .John (2005)

The homecoming by Jack Winter (1997)

Will your prodigal come home by Jeff Lucas (2007)

YouTube video clip

Prodigal Skit by the Skit Guys
https://youtu.be/HyVlF24u5dY

Chapter 5

The wall of blessing

What is the wall of blessing?

The wall of blessing is a prophetic picture of how by praying blessing over people and places daily, we can build a spiritual wall of blessing which is also a protection for our nation. This is not a physical wall but a spiritual prophetic wall.

This wall can be built one person at a time and one blessing at a time, and each blessing is like a brick in the wall so each one added makes the wall longer and higher.

Foundations

It is important to get the right foundation to the wall of blessing so that the wall can be strong and stable.

Our one and true foundation is discovered when we meet with Jesus and ask Him into our lives. Then Jesus takes us by the hand and leads us to the Father. If there is a way, there always must be a starting point. It says in John 14:6, *"Jesus is the way, the truth and the life. No one comes to the Father except through me."*

Living stones

Once we have Jesus as our Saviour, we have a firm foundation on which to build. We ourselves are like living stones that are built up as we trust God, worship Him, and get to know Him better. Take a moment to read the following Bible passage and let the words speak to you.

The living stone and a chosen people

As you come to him, the living Stone—rejected by humans but chosen by God and precious to him—you also, like living stones, are being built into a spiritual house to be a holy priesthood, offering spiritual sacrifices acceptable to God through Jesus Christ. For in Scripture it says: "See, I lay a stone in Zion, a chosen and precious cornerstone, and the one who trusts in him will never be put to shame." Now to you who believe, this stone is precious. But to those who do not believe, the stone the builders rejected has become the cornerstone, and, "A stone that causes people to stumble and a rock that makes them fall." (1 Peter 2:4-8)

We have so far talked about foundations and living stones. Let's start thinking about these foundations and living stones and how they relate to the Father's love and building walls of blessing.

We read in Revelation 21:19 that, *"The foundations of the city walls were decorated with every kind of precious stone."* The most precious thing that we can have in our heart and life is God. To know Him. Do you know Him? Do you long to know Him more? He loves you and longs that you would get to know Him. We have the promise in James 4:8 ESV *"Draw near to God, and he will draw near to you."*

God lays the foundation for the wall of blessing. The picture we have is of the jewels being people who have surrendered their lives to God. In normal foundations you would have rubble. In the wall of blessing God has a layer of precious stones. The picture we see is of the cement of love holding the rubble and precious stones together. This forms the foundation and that is what we build the wall of blessing on.

We need to be wise about our foundations. What are we building on? Who are we building on? It is not about the focus being on us or anyone else. It is no longer about celebrity but about the one we celebrate. We celebrate Jesus and the love and care of the Father. Our foundation can be upon nobody else but Jesus. 1 Corinthians 3 highlights the way we can easily follow people, but God calls us to follow Him. We must watch out for celebrity culture even within the church. We all have our part to play building the wall of blessing and we need each other. One may plant, one may water, one may harvest. We all have gifts. We are all unique and will all reflect a particular aspect of God's heart in what we do and say. It is not about one person being better than another, or about one person being a success and another being a failure. It is being about the Father's business, and that is not quantifiable this side of eternity, for God looks at our heart and He loves us just as we are. His love is not earned. He loves us unconditionally. We should not compare ourselves with others but look to Him, follow His example and ask Him to lead us and guide us each step of the way. We need to see ourselves as God sees us and know that we are precious to Him. Words like 'failure' or 'worthless' are not words He would speak over your life. His words are love, encouragement, blessing and approval. When we grasp that He is for us not against us, the enemies lie's will be exposed.

Whatever our past experiences and our upbringing, God is more than able to lay His foundations in our lives to bring healing, hope, restoration, and a purpose. No one is too far away. The Father's love and blessing is there for all. His light illuminates so that He can bless us and help us.

Having built a firm foundation, the rest of the wall needs to be built well also, so it stands firm. Having started with God building the foundation, we need to continue with God building the wall. To do that, He uses every one of us as living stones (1 Peter 2). We need to surrender to Him and let Him speak through us to others by being a living blessing, i.e., living and speaking blessings every day – a life of love and blessing.

Our foundations should be built on the word of God, on what Jesus says and His teaching.

"Everyone then who hears these words of mine and does them will be like a wise man who built his house on the rock. And the rain fell, and the floods came, and the winds blew and beat on that house, but it did not fall, because it had been founded on the rock. And everyone who hears these words of mine and does not do them will be like a foolish man who built his house on the sand. And the rain fell, and the floods came, and the winds blew and beat against that

house, and it fell, and great was the fall of it." (Matthew 7:24-27 ESV)

When we build on the word, this is a sure foundation. For those who have a prophetic gifting it is so important that we exercise this prayerfully and carefully, being sensitive to timing and the leading of the Holy Spirit.

Part of our foundation is to bless God for who He is without asking anything of Him. We bless Him because we love Him and delight to worship Him for who He is and what He has done for us.

The bricks are the blessings that build others up and the things we do to be a blessing. God is the wise builder. God calls us to look after ourselves and care for others. To be built up by His blessings so we can build up others.

"By the grace God has given me, I laid a foundation as a wise builder, and someone else is building on it. But each one should build with care. For no one can lay any foundation other than the one already laid, which is Jesus Christ. If anyone builds on this foundation using gold, silver, costly stones, wood, hay, or straw, their work will be shown for what it is, because the Day will bring it to light. It will be revealed with fire, and the fire will test the quality of each person's work. If what has been built survives, the builder will receive a reward. If it is burned up, the builder will suffer loss but yet will be saved — even though only as one escaping through the flames.

Don't you know that you yourselves are God's temple and that God's Spirit dwells in your midst? If anyone destroys God's temple, God will destroy that person; for God's temple is sacred, and you together are that temple." (1 Corinthians 3:10-17)

Broken down walls

Sometimes walls are broken down where we live. We have the wonderful story of the walls in Jerusalem being rebuilt. You may be sad about all sorts of things that happening around you, or even in your own situation. The good news is God longs to build up and bless. He rebuilds and restores.

Isaiah 58:12 says, *"Your people will rebuild the ancient ruins and will raise up the age-old foundations; you will be called Repairer of Broken Walls, Restorer of Streets with Dwellings."*

When a wall is breached it leaves a gap. This can have all sorts of consequences. Isaiah 61 not only speaks of rebuilding the ancient ruins but promises that the places that have been devastated will be restored. That ruined cities will be renewed. A prophetic picture is a wall with a big gap in where it has been destroyed; the bricks from it are not able to be used, so God puts a new thing in there. This is hope fulfilled, which is a blessing. This bridges the good things God has built in the past, connecting them to the good thing God is doing now, and also in the future, which turns it into a part of the wall of blessing.

Question

Maybe there are things broken down in your life and where you live. God longs to build these up. Take a few moments to bring to Father God the things that come into your mind that need to be rebuilt.

Individual blessings

We start by declaring blessings over our own lives. Often people feel selfish by blessing themselves and feel that they should not do it. However, the second commandment is to love others as ourselves. This shows that we cannot love others unless we love ourselves, and that the measure we love ourselves will be the measure we love others. In this context, we can't bless others until we have been blessed ourselves.

As we stand on God's word, applying it to our own lives, we will receive His blessing.

"I pray that God the Father and our Lord Jesus Christ will be kind to you and will bless you with peace! Christ obeyed God our Father and gave himself as a sacrifice to our sins to rescue us from this evil world. God will be given glory forever and ever. Amen." (Galatians 1:3-5 CEV)

The prayer of Jabez is a verse in the Bible that became a phenomenon a few years ago and inspired Christians to ask God to bless them. It is found in 1 Chronicles 4:10:

"Jabez cried out to the God of Israel. 'Oh that you would bless me and enlarge my territory! Let your hand be with me, and keep me from harm so that I will be free from pain.' And God granted his request."

Maybe this is a way that you could ask God to bless you personally. The last sentence in this verse shows God wants us to ask Him to bless us and that His answer is YES!

We need to realise that God wants to bless us as individuals and that we need to have that wall around us which is both a protection and enables us to able to bless other people, just as God tells us to love our neighbours as ourselves. Until we know what it is like to be blessed by God, we don't know how to declare blessings over others.

Rhythm of blessing and devotion

The rhythm of blessing is like the tide that flows in and out in our day. As we receive blessing from God, so blessing flows from us to others.

How do you feel about asking God to bless you?

Blessing can be an adventure and comes from a relationship with God.

Here are some questions that you may use to invite God into your day.

- What shall we read today?
- What shall we do today?
- What do you want to show me today?
- What do you want me to bless today?
- What do you want me to pray today?

It is easy to take for granted all the blessings we do have, and we may not even notice them. There is an old song called "Count your blessings". There is a line in it that says that you will be surprised by what God has done. Below we have written some blessings that we may take for granted.

Examples of counting blessings

Blessing

...of the joy of my salvation
...of a new day
...of eternal hope
...of shelter
...of food
...of the seasons
...of smiles
...of good memories
...others

Praying and declaring blessings over people, places and situations is one of the most loving things you can do. As we do, we invite God into people's situations, helping them fulfil their God-given destiny and be all that God has made them to be. Praying for others is asking for things they need and for God to intervene in their lives for their good. Speaking blessings is hearing what God wants to bless and do in their lives and declaring it over them. It is coming into agreement with God and declaring His heart for the person, place or situation being blessed. Praying in intercession is asking God for His best for the person, place, or situation and for His will to be done in their life, whilst declaring blessing is declaring God's blessing over the person place or situation, having already heard from God what it is He wants to bless and come into being.

Blessing people needs to become a way of life. If declaring blessings and being a blessing by what we say and do is one of the most loving things we can do, then we will want to build a wall of blessing round those closest to us. We do this, as we have learnt to live a life being blessed by God ourselves and receiving those blessings, by declaring blessings over those closest to us daily. This will be our family; to start with it might be our immediate family such as grandparents, parents, siblings, husband/wife, our children, and grandchildren. Later we might want to extend that to include our extended family; cousins, aunts and uncles and in-laws.

When we bless others or places, we are standing in the gap for them, and they receive the blessing. On 'This Morning', a TV programme, the presenters were playing a game called 'spin to win' with a caller who was having problems with their phone. They stood in the gap for the caller by answering the question to win extra goods, and so the caller was blessed by winning the extra prize. This is a good illustration of what we do when we declare blessings over people and places and we build a wall of blessing round them.

The language of love and blessing is a heart to heart connect. We share what the Father has given us from His heart so that others can receive that for themselves and do likewise with others. Two visual aids to help explain this could be a waterfall of blessing or ripples of blessing spreading out.

God is doing something new and building a wall of blessing around our nation. Part of that building may be rebuilding walls that are broken down that God had already put there. Where despair has taken place, God wants to bring hope and fill in the gap left by loss and grief. Where people are isolated and not part of their community God longs for them to be blessed and enjoy the company of others. For the lonely to be in friendship and fellowship. God places the lonely in families. God wants us to understand what family truly means, as God's people care for each other and others. Where people are struggling to meet their needs on a day to day basis, God longs to provide for people like a good Father so they can flourish in every way, enjoying life. Hope opens our eyes to the blessings around us and the blessing of other people we know. Hope and blessing go hand in hand, and when we are blessed we receive hope; we then can share that blessing of hope with others. God's heart is to establish us and bless us but also to heal and restore. Life has its broken places. You may have broken places. God knows about these things. In our life journey as we walk with Father God,

He will work in these areas to rebuild and build us up in His love. This is our hope.

As you bless you become a repairer of broken walls. Where are the broken walls in your family, community, and nation? Spend some moments writing down some of your thoughts. A name, a situation, a concern. Take what you have written to God and ask Him how to bless those people, situations and concerns you have.

Repairing broken walls

This is some words Lisa received about repairing broken walls.

"Daughter, I want you to pause and listen. Harken. Hear my voice. Prepare to repair the broken walls. Stand in the position I have given you and build up. Do not tear down. Build up through encouragement. Build up through time. Build up through your presence. Build up by listening. Build up by sharing vision. Build up by affirming. Build up by prophesying. Yes prophesying. Eat my scroll. Digest it and speak it...."

Within the UK we have counties, cities, towns, and villages. A wall of blessing can be formed around of each of these. God tells us to *"seek the welfare of the city where I have sent you into exile, and pray to the LORD on its behalf, for in its welfare you will find your welfare"*. (Jeremiah 29:7 ESV)

Where we live may be not where we work, and we can bless both places. We may have a job that takes us all over the country and the world, and we can bless wherever we go. Joshua 1:3, *"I will give you every place where you set your foot, as I promised Moses."* This promise was given to Joshua but has a spiritual application to us today as Jesus is with us wherever we go.

How do you feel about blessing others?

Honouring God and others as we bless is important. Building a wall of blessing will protect whatever or whoever it surrounds. This is because it is Father God's protection and has authority from Him.

Blessing together with others

For those of us who believe and trust in Jesus we are part of the body of Christ. Each person is precious, and we need each other. We are living stones that can build up our neighbourhoods. There are so many gifts we have been blessed with that we can share individually and together to bless others as part of ongoing care and outreach in our communities.

Take some moments to thank God for all the different ways Christians are blessing others by coming together. Write down things that you can think of in your church, between churches and in your community. Can you think of any new ways that you can bless together with others?

Sometimes we can get despondent as we have not seen much fruit. Sometimes there is a time for things to end, but other times God would say to us "let down the net again" as we seek Him. Even though we may feel there is no point, we are obedient and in this there is such a blessing of being in His will and waiting upon all He would do in us, as well as those we seek to serve and reach out to.

The original picture for the wall of blessing Wendy received was around the coast of the nation like an outline to the nation. This was a prophetic picture, and it was a spiritual wall rather than a physical wall. This wall can be built up by blessings being prayed every day. This can be done either virtually or by being physically present and blessing the land.

For example, when the pandemic in 2020 occurred, the annual London Prayer Loop walk became virtual as well as physical. A monthly Zoom call has gathered people together as a community to bless London and to pray for London, in addition to the ongoing physical established prayer walk.

A prophetic picture encouraging us to pull together

Lisa had a picture of people spread out along the shore pulling up a huge net of blessing. As we pull together in whatever God has laid on our hearts, His blessings will be revealed as the net is pulled onto shore. It takes everyone to do their bit for this to happen. There are still many more blessings that are to be revealed as we bless together.

Blessing different areas

Daily you might want to speak blessings over the place you live. You may also have a heart for a particular setting such as rural, urban or coast, which you might like to bless as well. Maybe when you are out in these places or are on holiday you could bless them then.

Blessing the rural

Our nation is blessed by the farmers who faithfully work the land so that we are provided with food. Farmers need the Father's blessing so that they can get a fair price for what they produce and so that they will have wisdom on how to farm the land they have. Harvest festivals over generations have been a way to thank God for the blessing of the harvest.

Take a moment to thank God for all those who farm our land so that we are blessed with food to eat.

Blessing the urban

Our nation is blessed by those who live in our urban communities. Each person precious and loved. Take a moment to thank God for all the blessings from our urban communities.

Wherever people live, there will be challenges and difficulties. Let us make the most of the opportunities given to us to encourage, support and share the love of Jesus wherever we go.

Blessing the coast

With the original vision of a prophetic spiritual wall of blessing around the nation it is so important that we bless the coast, both looking outwards and looking inwards. Blessing those who live along the coast and looking inwards into the nation. Blessing outwards means blessing those who enjoy the sea or work on the sea. Thanking God for all the blessings of the sea and blessing any nations across the sea from where you are standing.

Prophetic pictures of the wall of blessing

Wendy had a prophetic picture of the wall of blessing being like a sheep pen, keeping the nation safe. The map of the UK looks like a tower, so if the wall of blessing is a strong tower, a blessing from God, people can run into it. We build a wall of blessing around ourselves, our family, our home, our friends, our street, our town, our county, and our nation. Don't just say a blessing, be a blessing. The wall of blessing is like the Father's embrace, as it is not restrictive and does not need doors in or out; it is a moveable expression of His love and blessing upon our life. So, walking and speaking blessings as you walk along the coast is a way of building a foundation for the wall which is built higher by every blessing that is declared daily.

In Nehemiah it talks about each family being responsible for building the wall that is in front of them. In the context of what we have spoken about, that would mean saying blessings daily over the city, town, or village where you live and being a blessing in the way you relate to others. Whether you live in a rural, urban or coast situation, issues of despair, fear, poverty, and isolation will exist. God calls us to build up our communities in care blessing those we live amongst.

Write down some of the blessings that you have received from rural, urban and the coast.

Nations

Nations are a reward. Jesus was given nations as His reward. Nations are an extension of God's family. Even if nations do not get on, they are still part of His family. He blesses people with nations, and He also forms nations from people (Abraham). We have a parental responsibility from God for nations. To steward well and to care for those within the nations, acting justly and fairly. Sadly, this does not always happen, but we can make a difference by speaking blessings over nations and being a blessing in whatever way we have opportunity. We pray from the Father's heart, praying over the nation as we spend time with Him and receive His love for us. God loves and is as passionate over nations as with individuals.

Just like people may have a redemptive gift from their birth, nations may also have a redemptive gift. However nations might have gone away from God and not use their God given gift. God wants to restore these nations to himself. Sometimes this gift is called out. Just as we talk of seeing gold in people, we can see the 'gold' in nations and call out their redemptive gift. You may find it helpful to think about the Godly national/cultural foundations in the nations. He sees each nation, its redemptive gift and what He called the nation to at its beginnings. We have gone away from our beginnings. So far away from that now, and God wants to restore us to Him. Not just by name but by heart, leading individuals in that nation to know Him and believe and trust in Him.

We can bless others and still have different opinions over things. God commands a blessing where there is unity. This does not necessarily mean uniformity. God has made us unique, and we may have different perspectives. However, the one thing that does unite us is our belief and trust in Jesus. That He saves and that He cares for nations. That we are part of His plan to bless others, wherever they may be and whoever they are.

Where there are differences of opinion about nations and in nations, love will hold things together as we choose to bless others in the challenges. The language of blessing builds bridges and can bring reconciliation. To bless a nation, we also need to bless the leaders of a nation. We can build a political wall of blessing using the language of love with our MPs in our correspondence and when we meet them. We can speak blessing over our MPs and leaders in a daily blessing if we choose to do so, and you may like to send a card with a blessing to them. This does not mean we agree with some of the things they do. There are leaders who are tyrants, but God still asks us to bless. It is important to remember that this teaching in the Bible was written at a time when there were Christians in captivity and experiencing persecution and even death.

We have already mentioned earlier in this book how in the Second World War there was a ministry of information that assessed the morale of the people. This helped the government target a response. In many ways, the ministry of blessing can similarly help people and places where negative words and messages have made an impact. They are a kingdom response, bringing light in the darkness, building up walls that are broken down in our communities and in our nation. Blessing brings healing and transformation.

Walls as borders

The Macmillan Dictionary defines borders as "the official line separating two countries or regions". (Lisa) A few years ago I was prayer walking the Sandstone Trail in Cheshire. There is a part of the walk which is alongside a canal. The other side of the canal is Shropshire. When I was prayer walking there, I felt God lay it on my heart that when you bless the borders your borders will be enlarged. Another way of looking at this is when you bless a border God expands your heart to love the place, county, or nation.

It is important to speak blessings over borders, whether national or regional, because borders have often been associated with identity and regional or national pride. It is good to love where you live, but God calls us to affirm others and where they live. Not to hold a grievance, but to give to God anything that we struggle with, whether past or present, asking Him to bring His light and love into these things. Psalm 147:14 says, *"He grants peace to your borders and satisfies you with the finest of wheat."* As we give God our best, He gives us His best. He grants us peace and gives us the finest of fare. He even prepares a table in the presence of our enemies. A blessing that is beyond our imaginings. Peace is the best blessing of a nation. Peace can be in our heart, but it also can be peace on the land where there are no wars. Isaiah 60:18 says, *"No longer will violence be heard in your land, nor ruin or destruction within your borders, but you will call your walls Salvation and your gates Praise."* The amazing blessing of being a Christian is that even in time of war and in places where there is war, we can know the blessing of God's peace. A peace beyond all understanding. Even if there are natural fears, at the heart of who we are we can be anchored in Him.

It is so important to honour God in what we do and say because when we do, we are blessed. When a nation or region does not do this, blessing is withheld. A nation is made up of people and our actions can bring about blessing or hinder it. Isaiah 26:15 says *"O Lord, you have made our nation great; yes, you have made us great. You have extended our borders, and we give you the glory!"*

Places to build a wall of blessing

The main vision and one of the reasons this book was written is to see a wall of blessing around the coastline of the UK. Everything within this border is to have a wall of blessing around it, so the UK becomes blanketed by the Father's Blessing. The most important thing about this wall of blessing is that it comes from God the Father's heart and is based on the Father's love. The wall starts with an individual blessing, with a wall of blessing around you and everything concerning you. This means you can then build a wall of blessing around others. You might start with your husband or wife and then include your family. The other places that a wall of blessing can be built are: around streets, around schools, playschools, nurseries, colleges, universities, hospitals, doctor's surgeries, churches, ministries, Sunday schools, youth groups, businesses, shops, towns, villages, cities, counties, care homes, residential homes, police stations, fire stations, entertainment venues and so on. In fact, anywhere God loves is a place to build a wall of blessing around. Over all of these is a wall of blessing around the coast of the UK. With all these walls of blessing, our nation will be blessed and the people within it.

Physical wall of blessing inside church

Churches could have a wall of blessing as a physical wall where people can write blessings or write things that they would like to see blessed. These blessings could be scriptural blessings or ones God gives to you. The Father's Blessing can be written on it. As people learn to build walls of blessing, more and more blessings will be added onto this physical wall. One of the most familiar scriptural blessings is the Aaronic Blessing found in Numbers 6:24-26 which says, *"The Lord bless you and keep you; the Lord make his face to shine on you and be gracious to you; the Lord turn his face toward you and give you peace."* There could also be written details about how to build a wall of blessing around places and people for people to refer to. In essence, the wall of blessing is similar to a prayer wall that might be found in a church, but it is a blessing wall where the focus is on blessing.

After praying for a while God gave Wendy this picture: He showed that we had started to build the wall of blessing, but it was at the level of a toddler walking along the top of it with their hand being held by their father. However, as more blessings were being declared the wall was getting taller and taller. Eventually it reached heaven. As it did heaven came to earth and God's glory was brought down in it. It shimmered in the sun and was so bright you could almost not look at it. The light was all around the coast and was shining into the towns nearby. The streets were dark but the light from the wall shone into them, and it was as if night became day. The light was going into each of the streets and houses and passing from one house to another, so that as one house was lit up with the Father's love and blessing it was passed onto the next house and whole streets were lit up with the glory of God.

As Wendy and I discussed this picture, we felt it was connected to every street, home and person being blessed and coming to know the Father's love and blessing.

As we bless our streets, our towns, our neighbourhood, and our communities, we can also bless our families and others laid on our heart. It is like a blanket that covers the nation, a weighted blanket that calms anxiety and drives out fear. Each person is important and needed. Everyone working together builds up the wall. It comes out of a living relationship with Father God and each other. Hebrews 10:24, *"And let us consider how we may spur one another on toward love and good deeds."* As blessings are spoken or declared, lives are built up and God's kingdom is brought to earth. People come into their identity and become all God has purposed and planned, together and individually. The lies of the enemy are exposed, and the truth of God's love and care is made known.

What is in your hand?

(Lisa) The words, "What is in your hand?" have challenged me time and time again. It is so easy to get despondent when we look around us and wonder what we can possibly do. The need is so great. And yet, if we give God all that we are: our time, our gifts, our family, our brokenness, our illness, somehow He transforms and does more than we can ask or imagine. I often wonder what it must have been like to rebuild the wall in Nehemiah's time. Are our hearts sad like Nehemiah's was? Are we willing to work with others side by side, shoulder to shoulder? Only then can the walls be rebuilt. God commands a blessing when we dwell in unity. Are we willing to rebuild or are we waiting for others to do it for us? It is so easy to have a critical spirit and do nothing. Are we willing to get our hands dirty and make a difference with what is in our hand? Do we stand and watch? Getting bitter, getting fearful, and getting judgemental? Or do we prayerfully give God all that we are and ask Him to help us build up our families, our communities, and our nation. Do we release all that we are into His service? That God would help us get better not bitter. That He would cast out all fear and that He would help us let go of judgement. We must not despise the day of small things. Jesus took the bread and the small fish off the disciples, and He gave thanks before distributing them. God multiplied what was in their hand. *"Jesus is the same yesterday and today and forever."* (Hebrews 13:8). Show us Lord what is in our hands and help us to give these things to you, that you would use them for your glory. Amen.

Below are a few words God gave Wendy about a wall of blessing:

A wall of blessing - Keeps you safe inside.

A wall of blessing - Where you can hide.

A wall of blessing - Surrounds you with love.

A wall of blessing - A gift from God above.

A wall of blessing - Surrounding you.

A wall of blessing - What will you do?

A wall of blessing - Will you bless too?

A wall of blessing - Leading to breakthrough.

A wall of blessing - Around the world.

A wall of blessing - God's love unfurled.

A wall of blessing.

In the chapter of the prodigal son, we talk about the father's house in the story being like Father God's house. The reason I have written more about this here is because God showed me that as we build a wall of blessing around ourselves, others and various places, we are building the His house.

GOD THE FATHER'S HOUSE IS A HOUSE OF BLESSING. It is a large place full of rooms. Jesus says *"Do not let your hearts be troubled. You believe in God; believe also in me. In my father's house are many rooms; if that were not so, would I have told you that I am going there to prepare a place for you? And if I go and prepare a place for you, I will come back and take you to be with me that you also may be where I am."* (John 14:1-3)

Father God's house is a place where parties are held, and it is full of fun and laughter and joy. Jesus did his first miracle at a wedding, and we are told in Luke 15:7, *"there will be more rejoicing in heaven over one sinner who repents."*

Zephaniah 3:17 says, *"The Lord your God is with you, the Mighty Warrior who saves. He will take great delight in you; in his love he will no longer rebuke you, but will rejoice over you with singing."*

As in the parable, our father's house is a place of provision, as God is a father who provides for us. David elaborates, saying that God's people, *"feast on the abundance of your house, and you give them drink from the river of your delights"* (Psalm 36:8)

As with the house in the parable, it is an inclusive place where everyone is welcome. *"In my father's house are many rooms. If it were not so, would I have told you that I go to prepare a place for you? And if I go and prepare a place for you, I will come back and take you to be with me that you also may be where I am."* (John 14:2-3)

Jesus also said: *"Father, I desire that they also, whom you have given me, may be with me where I am, to see my glory that you have given me because you loved me before the foundation of the world."* (John 17:24 ESV). This also shows Father God's house is full of His glory, which is His love and blessing, the very essence of who He is.

Father God's house is a place of joy as it is the place where our father lives. Psalm 16:11 says *"You make known to me the path of life; you will fill me with joy in your presence, with eternal pleasures at your right hand."*

Father God's house is a house of blessing and Psalm 84:4 says, *"Blessed are those who dwell in your house..."*

Unsurprisingly, Jesus had a longing for his father's house talking about the temple, *"And he said to them, 'Why were you looking for me? Did you not know that I must be in my father's house?'"* (Luke 2:49 ESV).

He also said about the temple, *"It is written, 'My house shall be called a house of prayer,' but you make it a den of robbers."* (Matthew 21:13 ESV)

"Jesus answered him, 'If anyone loves me, he will keep my word, and my Father will love him, and we will come to him and make our home with him.'" (John 14:23 ESV). This shows that we are also Father God's house.

The psalms of David are filled with a longing to live in God's presence, within His house. In Psalm 26:8 ESV, David declares, *"O LORD, I love the habitation of your house and the place where your glory dwells."* In Psalm 27:4 ESV, David says, *"One thing have I asked of the LORD, that will I seek after: that I may dwell in the house of the LORD all the days of my life, to gaze upon the beauty of the LORD and to inquire in his temple."* In Psalm 84:1 ESV, David writes, *"How lovely is your dwelling place, O LORD of hosts!*

Some words Lisa received about the wall of blessing

"You ask me what the wall of blessing is? It is made up of living stones. People who live to bless. Who look for moments in their day when they can speak blessing, recognising the places where these words need to be spoken".

Going deeper

Start to build a wall of blessing round yourself, your family, your home, and street.
Start to build a wall of blessing round your town, your county, and the nation.
Read about building a wall in Nehemiah.

Decide to build a wall of blessing and please let us know that you are building a wall and where, so we know where the wall is being built.

Letter

My dear child,

As you build a wall of blessing based on my Father's blessing around yourself, you find yourself in the Father's house. The Father's house is where I am. My presence fills the house, and my house is a place of love and blessing. The walls are my Father's blessing and contained inside is my Father's love, a perfect, unconditional love. You cannot move inside my house without feeling my love. The atmosphere consists of everything I am, and you have never experienced anything like it elsewhere. This is where you start living a life of love and blessing. Soak it in, enjoy it, it is for each of my children. In this place you can live day to day with me. All my children can live here, and as you build a wall of blessing round those you love, round people, places, and even entire nations, they begin to experience my Father's house and thus my Father's love and blessing. So why not start building that wall of blessing right now and see the difference that you make by doing so. I long for you to live with me surrounded by my love and blessing. I love you.

Love, your Dad, Almighty God.

Prayer

Father before I can bless, I need to receive your blessing for me. Before I can give a blessing, I need to receive from you. Help me be still and be open to what you will say through your word. Help me sit at your feet and enjoy spending time with you. Help me count my blessings and find you in all circumstances. Amen

Blessing

Be blessed to build a wall of blessing around those things that are personal to you. Be blessed to build a wall of blessing around larger areas such as town, county or nation, and find others to join you in blessing these things.

Songs

For I am building a people of power by Dave Richards (1975)
Count your blessings by Guy Penrod (2012)
Build my Life by Pat Barrett sung also by Michael W Smith and others (2018)

Books

Releasing heaven on earth by Alistair Petrie (2000)
The kingdom belongs to Little children by Barry Adams (2016)
40 days of Love by Wendy Thomas (2014)

Resources

Virtual Prayer Walking Guide (digital) –
www.neighbourhoodprayer.net/resources/

Chapter 6

Lifestyle of love and blessing

The lifestyle of love and blessing is one God wants everyone to experience. This is the lifestyle that Adam and Eve lived when they were in the Garden of Eden before the fall. They lived loved, and were blessed by God, walking with Him as His children, sharing everything and walking in the authority that God gave them. They knew nothing but love and blessing from God and each other, and walked with God every day, sharing their lives with Him. This was God's plan for human lives, and by the death of Jesus for our wrongdoings, we can be restored to this lifestyle.

Relationship

The lifestyle of love and blessing is about relationship. It is about our relationship with God and His relationship with us, and about our relationship with others. God is blessed every time we talk to Him, every moment we spend with Him, every conversation when we tell Him we love Him. In our natural relationships, we can bless others by the way we talk to them, the time we give them and the love we share with them. It is a blessing to know we are not alone, and that God is with us continually throughout our day, every day. Psalm 23 tells us His goodness and mercy follow us each day of our lives. He is the good shepherd. He looks out for us and is there when we get lost or fall. He longs to bring His love and blessing to us when we are hurting in any way. And He longs that we are able to bless others in His name. When we bless others, we introduce them to God's love for them.

It is only as we know God as our Father and live our lives from that relationship saturated with His love for us, knowing His blessing, that we can be free to live the lifestyle of love and blessing. Once we know that kind of lifestyle, we are free then to bless others and share the Father's love.

Walking with God as Father, knowing His love and blessing for us personally and being able to give that away, enables us to live the abundant life that Jesus talked about.

A lifestyle of blessing encompasses every area of your life. It is not restricted to religious activities but also impacts creativity, sport, work, education, language, relationships, responsibilities, housework, interests, and hobbies. Nothing is left out. God's blessings for us are available whatever time of day or night. There may be times when you have difficulty sleeping, but God's blessings are still available for you even then.

I am reminded of a song from the musical *The King and I* called "Getting to Know You". It speaks of spending time with someone and then knowing what to say as the relationship grows. As we spend time with God, we are then able to bless others from a place of understanding more of the Father's love for ourselves and others which impacts what we say and do.

Sow a blessing

As we spend time with God, sowing words of scripture of God's love and care into our hearts, each day these will overflow in what we do and say. As we receive the blessings in God's word and in any other way God speaks to us, we can share these blessings with others. 2 Corinthians 9:6 ESV says, *"whoever sows sparingly will also reap sparingly, and whoever sows bountifully will also reap bountifully."*

Say a blessing

This includes speaking blessings over neighbours, friends, work colleagues or your family and using the language of love and blessing in our conversation as we have opportunity.

Be a blessing

We can be open to ways of blessing others through words of encouragement, friendship, and acts of kindness.

Share the blessing

The most important blessing anyone can ever receive is hearing about Jesus and coming to know Him and God as Father. As we have opportunity, we can share our faith and what God has done in our lives and the lives of others.

Identifying people and places to bless

We have put together below a list of people and places that you may like to bless. You may like to add to it. When you read through the list, see if there is anything that moves you to bless. God's heart is to bless people in every sphere of life, but not always every activity that they undertake or engage with.

NHS, surgeries, ambulance service, hospitals, prisons, schools, government, local council, police, fire, nursing homes, churches, ministries, business, farming, universities, colleges, night-time economy (pubs, clubs, restaurants, theatres, and cinema), sports, arts, music, and entertainment.

Here is an example how to bless the NHS:

I bless all the people that serve in the NHS whether cleaners, porters, surgeons, doctors, nurses, pharmacists, administrators, or maintenance staff, that they would have the strength to cope with all that is happening each day.

Sometimes we may struggle to bless if we feel negative or critical about a particular group of people. For example, we may say we do not like politicians. This immediately creates a barrier to blessing. We may not agree with the decisions they make but we can choose to bless. We can say we are praying for them. In any communications we can show care and consideration, not only about the issues that concern us but for them as people.

Blessing situations and events

We can bless events such as national elections or we can bless in times of crisis. Blessing brings peace into tense situations and enables God's voice to be heard. When people bless it does not inflame what is happening

Personal Blessing Buddies

You may like to consider blessing someone you know well for confidentiality and safe-guarding. Agree with each other to stay in touch over a period and pray for each other and bless each other. Find creative ways to make each person's day better. You may like to bless for twenty-one days or forty days or on an ongoing basis. We are blessed in giving and receiving, so this is a double blessing, recognising what God has given you and giving it away. Let's look at two scriptures:

> Matthew 10:7-8, *"And as you go, preach, saying, "The kingdom of heaven is at hand." Heal the sick, cleanse the lepers, raise the dead, cast out demons. Freely you have received, freely give."*
>
> Mark 16:20, *"Then the disciples went out and preached everywhere, and the Lord worked with them and confirmed his word by the signs that accompanied it".*

Note that as people shared the love of God, the Lord worked with them, and signs accompanied what they shared. This is not brought about by our own hard work. This is the blessing of God working with us and through us, rather than us striving to work for God.

Community Blessing Buddies

Not only can we have personal blessing buddies, but we can have Community Blessing Buddies. This could be when a small group get together to bless each other from afar or in their own homes. This may be meeting on Zoom, or in person when allowed, sharing fellowship with each other. Community Blessing Buddies would be regularly communicating with each other to bless each other. They may have a group WhatsApp to encourage and support each other on a regular basis. Church could be a place where there could be intentional community blessing, which could be facilitated through established groups such as home groups, prayer groups and other groups. In its care of community and outreach, churches could also intentionally work with nursing homes to bless those who are isolated and lonely through activities such as letter writing, blessing cards and regular contact. There could be a blessing notice board where people can pin blessings that they have had as testimony and written blessings for others in the church including Bible verses. There could be written blessings for those who serve their community in a variety of areas.

Blessing Buddies in the workplace

You may or may not work in a Christian business or industry but wherever you work you can look out for people, speak words of encouragement and blessing into their lives. You can also declare blessings over the business and the way they work. You can pray for the owners, the managers and all staff and customers. You may get to know other Christians in your workplace and be a blessing buddy with them.

Our street and community

There is a purpose and plan for your life and where you live. Sometimes we can lose that connect because of all the other things that are happening in our life. Yet we have an opportunity to bless our neighbours and streets if we choose to do so. We can intentionally bless those on our doorsteps. Take some time now to bless your home, your neighbours, and your street. God loves your household and those who you live amongst. His heart is to bless people with His love. People are blessed when we are interested in them and speak words of blessing into their lives. They are blessed when we ask how they are. They are blessed when we listen to them. They are blessed when we are there for them when they need us. Most people are blessed when we ask whether we can pray for them.

However sometimes we need to give people their space and privacy. Other times people can feel isolated and alone and need our presence and the blessing of our company. We in turn will be blessed by spending time with them. We need to ask God for discernment as to when to be there and when to give people space. We need to pray for wisdom and sensitivity and God's perfect timing. Blessing those in your street and community is declaring blessings over them every day and blessing them in practical ways when appropriate. It is joining in with and initiating good relationships where you live that will bless those around you as well as receiving the blessing of being part of a community where you live. Be open to ways God would encourage you to bless them and get to know them. Ask God what is on His heart for where you live? Ask Him to show you what the issues are? Ask God to show you how to bless in response?

If you know the names of your neighbours spend some moments speaking blessings over them. If you do not know their names speak blessings over the homes near to where you live.

Street blessing

Street blessing is not only blessing homes. It is blessing all that is good and wholesome that happens on your street, whilst also praying for the things that concern you. Streets can have bad names and reputations and we can speak another word of blessing over these places, believing and trusting God to transform them. We can also thank God for the blessing of streets where community is thriving and bless what is happening. As we do this, we see things in a different way and view others in a different way. This transforms us as much as the places we are blessing. God may place streets on your heart to bless. You may also have a natural affinity with a street. The street may be the place you work or the street on which your church is on. Or the streets of friends or family or somewhere that you have had a connect with in the past. Or a street of great need. There may be people who we know are regularly prayer walking particular streets for different reasons. They may be Street Pastors or Street Angels. We can bless them as we bless the streets on our heart. Every time you go out, speak a blessing over your street and all the people who live on your street.

Blessing your neighbourhood

You may like to strategically bless your neighbourhood by praying for your neighbours, caring for your neighbours, and sharing Jesus with your neighbours as you have opportunity, with the aim of seeing every street covered in prayer. To find out more visit www.neighbourhoodprayer.net

Sharing the Father's Love Letter

You may like to share the Father's Love Letter with people in your community. Speak blessings upon the people first and then the area in which you are delivering them. When you deliver the Father's Love Letter, aim to include an invite to something that will give opportunity to build a relationship with them or offer some practical act of care so they can see God's love and experience it for themselves.

Blessing walking

There is something special about going for a walk with someone you love and someone who loves you. This is what it is like as we walk out each day with Father God who loves us and wants to bless us. Sometimes we walk through difficult times and situations, and God is with us each step of the way. You may be familiar with the footprints reflection that showed one set of footprints in the sand during difficult times and the beautiful message that there was only one set of footprints because God was carrying that person through everything they were going through. Psalm 23:4, *"even though I walk through the darkest valley, I will fear no evil, for you are with me; your rod and your staff they comfort me."* When we have the Father's love with us it will take away all fear. God is there to rescue. God is there to protect, and God is there is to comfort. God has all authority.

You may be familiar with prayer walking, but you can also blessing walk too. Blessing walking is walking with your heavenly Father, allowing Him to show you things in any given area. Prayer walking and blessing walking are like non-identical twins and go hand in hand together for the wellbeing of people, places, and situations. People and places get God's input and are the beneficiaries of the prayers and declarations of blessings. There is an old song by Ralph McTell about being led through the streets in London. Well, God our Father wants to take us by the hand through not just London but every village, town, and city. Wherever you go. God wants us to walk with Him and to show us places and people from His perspective. God knows we will go into the countryside or coast to find beautiful things, but He can show us beautiful things in the urban too.

As you go out blessing walking with your heavenly Dad, you can listen to what He says and see what He wants you to see. You may go to the same place and see different things each time. Father God is standing with His hand outstretched saying "will you come for a walk with me?" Answer Him, then at the start of the walk ask Him questions such as OK, where are we going? Who are we going to meet today? What do you want to show me? What Bible verses do you want to share? What's on your heart? Then as you hear what He wants to be blessed, say blessings over these places and use the words you hear Him say. If you want sample blessings to use over various places there is a chapter later in the book you can use.

So many blessings come from this blessing walking: The blessing of being with your heavenly Father. The blessing of enjoying His creation. The blessing of seeing beauty in the urban. The blessing of listening. The blessing of meeting people along the way. Then the practical blessing of seeing what He wants being blessed. Almost like drawing back the curtains and seeing what God wants to show you for the place you live or the place you blessing walk.

In this season, blessing walking is what God wants to highlight and teach you if it is something you are not familiar with already. Prayer walking is accepted and practised by many Christians, but blessing walking is not so well known. God is standing in front of you with hands outstretched saying – come on let's go for a walk. He has got things He wants to show you. If you walk by yourself, you will not see it. You can only capture the Father's heart for places when you walk with Him and see places through His eyes. He will show you things you have not seen. Treasures in unexpected places as said in Isaiah 45:3: *"I will give you hidden treasures, riches stored in secret places. So that you may know that I am the Lord, the God of Israel, who summons you by name."* All these treasures are out there, and He wants you to see them. You would see them if you went for a walk with Him and as you capture His love for what He has created, whether country or urban or coastal. Walks in countryside are often about being blessed yourself, being renewed by scenery and counting your blessings as well as blessing the land and anyone you meet. Blessing walks in towns are about capturing the Father's love for people and His plans for a place. He has plans not only for individuals but places also.

Practical blessings of blessing walking

You do not just say blessings as you blessing walk but you can be a practical blessing as well. Being a blessing as you walk could mean doing a litter pick, practical care of the land. It may mean walking with others and talking to them, maybe praying with them, or saying a blessing over them. For example, in the Bible, the disciples on the Emmaus Road were walking with Jesus and He talked to them; you can spend time with someone, and they can spend time with you. This is a blessing for both of you.

Having others walking with us and journeying with people, we are able to share in that blessing by being there with them, listening, sharing, and supporting each other in our communities. You can also be a blessing by saying hello to a neighbour.

We should be excited about being with God and going for a walk with Him. We should go expectantly and with eyes open to bless.

If you were walking with a loving father, he would be saying things such as: Can you see this, can you see that? Can you see the sunset? Walking with Father God in blessing walking is the same type of experience.

Are you willing to have your plans interrupted? To say hello to someone? To go for a walk that you did not plan? It is an adventure with God.

Receive blessing on a blessing walk

You can be blessed by birdsong, beauty of nature, by busy urban places, by the blessing of the community around. Use all your senses: sight, hearing, smell, touch, and taste. Enjoy communion with God and others. Bless the land. Bless the atmosphere.

Find a new love for the nation in the land, the beauty of creation, the way God speaks through creation. God loves the ground and the animals as well as humans. God clothes the lilies of the field and so tells us not to worry. Jesus taught people through the land and creation.

I, Wendy, at autumn time, was up in Scotland. There was a breath-taking view of the mountain and trees. I said to my husband to pull over and stop and take some photos. The photos were not showing the fullness of the beauty and I was frustrated as I wanted to be able to share the beauty with others. You do not have to share everything, some things are just for you, and I heard God say to me: If you were the only person on the earth, I would still have created this scenery for you. This was just as much God's way of telling me He loved me as hearing it through a sermon, or a song or any way else. I have always enjoyed beautiful scenery, but I had not realised He would have created it just for me as an expression of His love. This was so precious to me, and I experienced God's love in a new way.

When I, Lisa, had major brain surgery I was not able to see the beauty of the countryside or much sky from my window for ten days. When I came out of hospital I burst in tears at the beauty of a blade of grass. It was like God opened my eyes to His creation. I had said a prayer in the past to God that I wanted to appreciate creation like others I knew, but through something difficult God answered my prayer and awakened my senses.

Blessing buddies might be walking with others i.e., walking with God and also with others. He is with you wherever you go. Wherever you walk should be a blessing walk and you can bless those behind the doors you pass. Every time you go out, speak a blessing over your street and everyone who lives or works in your street.

Everywhere you walk should be a walk with your heavenly Dad. When you fall in love you walk together. Just being together is everything. God loves going for a walk with us and showing us things. He loves showing us the beauty of creation but will also show us beauty wherever we go. God loves everywhere urban, rural and coastal. We may come across things that trouble and disturb us in the down and out places. In dangerous places, God is still walking with you and will show you things to bless. He is there showing you the gold in that place. He is showing you what matters and what is really important. He is there with you spiritually. He is there to show you what to do and how to bless. Sometimes you can only pick up what the Father is saying about a place or person as you walk the ground with Him. God is with us wherever we go whether in the countryside or in the city. He cares for creation, and He cares for those who live in urban environments.

Spending time with someone and enjoying each other's company during blessing walking is a way of you receiving blessing as well as being a blessing.

Letter

My dear child,

Will you come for a walk with me? will you let me show you things you have not seen before? Will you let me tell you what is on my heart? Will you take me by the hand and share time with me? Will you listen to what I say and speak my words over people and places? Will you bless what I bless? This time will be such a blessing to both of us as well as others. I love spending time with you. You are my precious child, and father and child time is always such fun and a sheer delight. Yes, I delight in you as I do in all my children. I love you and I love spending time with you. It makes me happy to see you catch my heart for people and places. So how about that walk?

Love, your Dad, Almighty God

Gateway blessing

In our daily lives there are times when we or others may need support. We thank God for the blessing of those who can help. When we or others are given information about how to connect with support, this is a gateway blessing. Are you aware of different local initiatives like food banks, debt support, mental health support etc. in your area that you could use or direct people to? Is there something you feel God may be leading you to do to bless others where you live?

Write down the things you could gateway people to in your area? What things could you find out about that would be useful to know?

What can you give to bless others?

Ask God what blessings could you give away to others. It may be your time. You might like to volunteer with a charity. It may be helping at church. It may be praying for someone. You may have a particular gifting that would bless someone. Maybe you are a cook and could bake a cake or a meal. Maybe you are an artist and could paint a picture or do a personal card of blessing. Maybe you are a gardener and could give a plant, flowers, vegetables, or fruit from your garden to bless someone. Maybe you could write down some of the things that come to your mind. These could also be a double blessing, as you have the joy of growing, baking, or creating something and others have the joy of receiving it.

God maybe calling you to share the blessing of who you are in Him with your neighbours. Do not hide your light under a bushel. God calls us to have a servant attitude not a ghetto mentality.

Blessing of fellowship

John 13:34-35 says *"A new commandment I give you: Love one another. As I have loved you, so you also must love one another. By this everyone will know that you are My disciples if you love one another."* When we truly love each other, we will cultivate a life in common, being careful what we do and say. We will honour and bless each other. We will prefer others, looking out for their interests. We will encourage. We will consider what we say and when we say it. It is not always easy, but as we pursue a life of integrity and love together, bearing with each other and forgiving each other, God will work. God is our Father, and He longs for us as His family to be as one. longs to bless us.

Acts 2:42-47 speaks of the fellowship of believers. It says *"They devoted themselves to the apostles' teaching and to fellowship, to the breaking of bread and to prayer. Everyone was filled with awe at the many wonders and signs performed by the apostles. All the believers were together and had everything in common. They sold property and possessions to give to anyone who had need. Every day they continued to meet together in the temple courts. They broke bread in their homes and ate together with glad and sincere hearts, praising God and enjoying the favour of all the people. And the Lord added to their number daily those who were being saved."*

Blessing of forgiveness

To live a lifestyle of love and blessing is to be going before God daily to say sorry for the things that are laid on your heart and receiving the blessing of forgiveness. When you are able to bless the person who has wronged you, God will work in your heart and will help you to fully forgive them. You may find the Lord's prayer helpful.

*"Our Father in heaven, hallowed be your name, your kingdom come, your will be done, on earth as it is in heaven. Give us today our daily bread. **And forgive us our debts, as we also have forgiven our debtors**. And lead us not into temptation, but deliver us from the evil one."* (Matthew 6:9-13)

Psalm 32:1 says, *"Blessed is the one whose transgressions are forgiven, whose sins are covered."* We are invited into a relationship with God where He will take all the things we have done wrong and bless us with His forgiveness. Isaiah 1:18 NLT says *"Come now, let's settle this"*, says the Lord. *"Though your sins are like scarlet, I will make them as white as snow. Though they are red like crimson, I will make them as white as wool."* It is because Jesus died on the cross and shed His blood for us and rose again that we can come into relationship with Jesus and come to know the Father. When we confess our sins, the guilt is taken away. We can find the blessing of peace. 1 John 1:8 says, *"If we claim to be without sin, we deceive ourselves and the truth is not in us. If we confess our sins, he is faithful and just and will forgive us our sins and purify us from all unrighteousness."*

When trials or tribulations come, we have the blessing of a hiding place in Him. A tower of refuge. Our Father surrounds us with songs of deliverance. He helps us and teaches us. He counsels us and watches over us. *"The Lord's unfailing love surrounds the man who trusts in him."* (Psalm 32:10) Whatever we are going through God is there with us. He is there through every challenge and difficulty. He is not our enemy. He is our good Father. He delights in us and loves us. He knows our circumstances. Every hair of our head is counted. We are blessed to know we are His delight. We are blessed to know He is our sanctuary. We are blessed to know He is our advocate. As we receive our Father's blessings for us, knowing we are loved, we are able to love others. We can love our neighbour. We can love our enemy by God's enabling. We can build up the places that are broken down with the sure foundation of knowing who we are in Christ. Our Father will help us know what to do and what to say. Integrity will be our guard and we will honour and prefer others. As we are attentive to the word and what it says, we will be able to discern what to do.

Blessing your enemy

When we bless our enemy or bless others who have different views to us, it is not that we agree with them, but we do believe God's heart is a heart of love and to bless. Blessing is not compromise. Blessing costs. Living loved and blessed. You personally receive love and blessing and then live a lifestyle of love and blessing, where your loving and blessing of others is coming out of your relationship of being loved and blessed. Both are important things to do, you cannot do loving and blessing others until you have been loved and blessed. Blessing is not that we come in agreement with everything to be a friend of everyone. It is not endorsement of someone or something, but it is a freely given gift of blessing them as a person because they are loved and precious. It is about unconditional blessing.

Prophetic blessings

Prophetic blessing is God's way of saying to people I see you, I know you, I love you and I see you as I always intended you to be. The best you, the real you, the way I created you (Psalm 139). I am totally in love with you, and I believe in you. The best is yet to come. I bless you with everything you need to fulfil your destiny, to leave a legacy and to be the wonderful person you really are. I give you my Father's blessing so nothing will hold you back. You have my covering and favour, authority and wisdom to step into your future, a wide open space full of possibilities. All my riches are yours, spend them wisely. Welcome home into my Father's heart. All that I am and have I give you. I withhold no good thing from you. Prophetic blessing is speaking out God's Father's heart for them.

For the nation, there could be a group of people who have a heart for the nation and seek God's heart for the nation, seeking it out in prophetic blessing. This may also be one nation blessing other nations.

Prophetic blessing is holding up a mirror into God's heart and reflecting it into a person's heart. It is saying the Father's blessing over them, and it is like a window into people's heart and spirit; God seeing them clearly and speaking out their destiny and the gold in them. It is also like a window into heaven but zooming into God's heart and spirit to see and know Him as He truly is and know His love.

Prophetic blessing is seeing in the spirit and using natural words to explain to people what is happening in the spirit and to make it real. It comforts and encourages, gives people wings and insight into themselves and their giftings and destiny. It is part of the wall of blessing. It calls out the gold in people and gives them a hope and future. It gives them a way forward without being directive. It will help people know that God knows everything about them and loves them as they are, and to see themselves as God sees them. It will bring back the prodigals, as they will know they are accepted and welcomed home. It will give people a sense of self-worth. It gives people a hope and a future as they see God's plans for them. It gives a purpose to them. It is not just for individuals but for nations, speaking out the gifting and purpose of the nations. It should be a natural thing and not scary.

Prophetic blessing does not just have to be words. It could be a picture, a heart or whatever. Prophecy is hearing what God says and telling others. Prophetic blessing is hearing God's heart for a person and telling them. It is a window into God's heart and a window into a person's heart.

142

It is always positive. The Father's Blessing is an example of prophetic blessing. It combines both prophesy and blessing, but it is different to both and more than the sum of both.

Some words Lisa received about giving away blessing

Give away my blessing to others and like the oil that was refilled, I will keep giving you more blessings to give away as you receive my blessing for you.

Going deeper

- Are you already living under the Father's love and blessing? If not, what can you do to start living this lifestyle?
- Do you show God's love and blessing to others around you? If not, how can you start doing this?

Letters

My dear child,

Do you know just how much I love to bless you? You are my precious child, the apple of my eye. I love you eternally and perfectly with an unconditional love. Love always wants to bless the loved one and I AM love. I want to bless you just because you are my child, and I am your Father. You do not have to earn my blessings; I give them to you freely. They are a gift of grace, yours to enjoy. I say to you, freely you have received so freely give. You can bless others in word and deed the same way I bless you. I bless you in every area of life, not grudgingly but willingly. It gives me great pleasure to bless you. I love seeing your happiness as you receive and enjoy my blessings. They are one more way I express my love for you. I bless you with abundant life, not just with meeting your needs but fulfilling your desires as well. Trust me and live your life within my love and blessings.

Love, Your Dad, Almighty God

My daughter,

Let me show you the full extent of my love. For this is my inheritance for you. A love that will not fail. A love that is unconditional. A love that covers over a multitude of sins. Let me teach you how to live a lifestyle of love, blessing others. My love was costly, and as you love it will cost. There are times of suffering, but as you go through troubles and tribulations my counsellor will be with you and you will know me ever present. You will be able to give testimony from all I do, and you will be able to love and support those going through suffering too. Selah.

Your Dad xxx

Prayer

Heavenly Father,
I want to live a lifestyle of love and blessing and know that is what you want for me also. Please help me to live this lifestyle and draw ever closer to you as my Dad. Amen

Blessing

Be blessed to live a lifestyle of love and blessing, where you live in the Father's love and blessing and give that away to others. Amen

Songs

Living in the Overflow video on YouTube by People & Songs. https://youtu.be/UyvbnbWfLV0
Arise & Shine by Here Be Lions (2018)
I am loved MackBrock [official lyric video]
https://youtu.be/9OmYhgvwQa8

Books

Experience the Father's Embrace by Jack Frost (2013)
Daddy you love me by Brent Lokker (2012)

Chapter 7

Blessing of family

God our heavenly Father loves to bless His children and we can see this from the beginning of the Bible in Genesis. What is also key is that He loves to bless families. Families are God's idea, and they are meant to be a blessing. Unfortunately, they are not always blessings in our fallen world, but do not give up hope because God is a God who restores and can restore broken families. We are told that God puts the lonely in families and you should never be lonely if you are part of God's family. Of course, God has already promised that He will never leave you. Joshua 1:5 *"I will never leave you or forsake you."* God blessed Adam and Eve as soon as He has created them as we see in Genesis 1:28 *"God blessed them and said to them "Be fruitful and increase in number; fill the earth and subdue it. Rule over the fish in the sea and the birds in the sky and over every living creature that moves on the ground."* As we see here, having children, i.e., increasing in number, is a blessing.

We are then told that Adam and Eve had two sons, Cain and Abel. The first dysfunctional family as Cain killed Abel. They then had another son called Seth. The next chapter in Genesis 5 is titled from Adam to Noah and describes Adams family line which resulted in Noah. Noah illustrates God's blessing to families and in Genesis 7:1 it says, *"The lord then said to Noah, 'Go into the ark, you and your whole family, because I have found you righteous in this generation.'"* The next two chapters detail what happened with the ark until it lands. Then in Genesis 9:1 we see God blessing Noah and his family *"Then God blessed Noah and his sons saying to them, 'Be fruitful and increase in numbers and fill the earth.'"* This is the same blessing given to Adam and Eve. Once again, we can see that families are meant to be a blessing and that God blesses families.

Genesis 10 and 11 describe the family line of Noah and his sons and how it results in Abram being born. Then Abram's family line is described and in Genesis 12:1-3 NKJV it says, *"The Lord had said to Abram, 'Go from your country, your people and your father's household to the land I will show you. I will make you into a great nation; and I will bless you. I will make your name great, and you will be a blessing. I will bless those who bless you, and whoever curses you I will curse; and all peoples on earth will be blessed through you.'"* In some translations, the final line in verse 3 says: *"And in you all the families of the earth shall be blessed."*. Also, in more modern translations it says all families will be blessed. This shows from the very beginning God intended to bless families and that families are meant to be a place of blessing.

Abrahamic blessing

Abraham is first mentioned right at the beginning of the Bible, and we are told of the covenant between Abraham and God and how God promises to not only bless Abraham but also all his descendants. We too now come under all the Abrahamic blessings, as we are told in Galatians 3:14, *"He redeemed us in order that the blessing given to Abraham might come to the Gentiles through Christ Jesus, so that by faith we might receive the promise of the Spirit."*

After God's blessing, other people are moved to bless Abram and in Genesis 14:19-20 we see a priest, Melchizedek bless Abram. He says: *"Blessed be Abram by God Most High, Creator of heaven and earth. And praise be to God Most High, who delivered your enemies into your hand."*

God has always seen children as a blessing and in Abram's time and culture it was seen even more so than today. Any child was a blessing and the more children you had, the more blessed by God you were seen to be; to be childless was a thing of shame. So, we see in Genesis 15:2 Abram complaining to God: *"But Abram said, 'Sovereign Lord, what can you give me since I remain childless and the one who will inherit my estate is Eliezer of Damascus?'"* God immediately reassures him saying, *"'This man will not be your heir; but a son who is your own flesh and blood will be your heir.' He took him outside and said 'Look up at the sky and count the stars, if indeed you can count them.' Then he said to him, 'So shall your offspring be.'"* (Genesis 15:4-5) Abram believed God and then God says, *"I am the Lord who brought you out of Ur of the Chaldeans to give you this land to take possession of it."* (Genesis 15:7) This passage shows the blessing of inheritance and having an heir to leave it to, and also the blessing of land and how God gives people land as a blessing.

In Genesis 16, Sarai is still childless, so she comes up with a plan with Abram to let him sleep with her maidservant and have a child with her. This happens and the maid gives birth to a son, Ishmael. In Genesis 17, God appears to Abram and makes a covenant with him, telling him he will be the father of many nations and be very fruitful, that He will make nations of him and that kings will come from him and that He will be his God and the God of his descendants. God also said He was changing his name to Abraham which is because He was making him father of many nations. God also said Sarai would have her name changed to Sarah. God said He would bless her and give Abraham a son by her who is to be called Isaac, and that she will be the mother of nations and kings of people will come from her. Then in Genesis 17:18 Abraham says, *"If only Ishmael might live under your blessing."* This shows how all children, whether legitimate or not, were valued and should be blessed. God agrees to bless Ishmael and says he will be fruitful and greatly increase his numbers. He would also be the father of twelve rulers and be made into a great nation. However, His covenant is with Isaac.

Abraham and Sarah do have a son whom they name Isaac, the Bible not only notes all that happens in Abraham's relationship with God but tells of his family line down through the generations and how God blesses them with the blessing He gave Abraham, simply because they are Abraham's children. In Genesis 26 we see God blessing Isaac. This is what He says in verse 3, *"Stay in this land for a while, and I will be with you and will bless you. For to you and your descendants I will give all these lands and will confirm the oath I swore to your father."* In verse 24: *"That night the Lord appeared to him and said, 'I am the God of your father Abraham. Do not be afraid, for I am with you. I will bless you; I will increase the number of your descendants for the sake of my servant Abraham.'"* Then in Genesis 28, we see God blessing Jacob who is Isaac's son and the grandson of Abraham. He is blessed by God as Isaac calls Jacob and blesses him with Abraham's blessing *"May he give you and your descendants the blessing given to Abraham, so that you may take possession of the land where you now reside as a foreigner, the land God gave to Abraham."* (Genesis 28:4) This carries on down the generations and is an example of generational blessing, showing the importance of parents blessing their children. There are blessings from previous generations that God uses to bless us in our generation.

(Lisa) I have been blessed to read some of the letters written by my relatives in the 19th Century that have spoken about their faith. This has been such an encouragement to know that they had a relationship with God.

Generational blessings do not only have to come in keepsakes and material blessings. They can be spiritual blessings, such as lessons people have learnt from God that they share with you. It can be the testimony of how they came to know Jesus and the way God works in their life. (Wendy) A much older lady in my church used to talk to me of all the things God had spoken to her and done in her life. She used to share Bible verses that meant a lot to her and how they had applied in her life. This lady is now with God but the blessing of the things she shared with me still remains.

Are there things in your life that are a generational blessing?

In Exodus God even identifies himself by saying 'I am the Lord the God of your fathers Abraham Isaac and Jacob'. God is a trigenerational God. He blesses your children and children's children because of His relationship with you. This is one of the blessings of being part of a family.

In the New Testament there are numerous references to Abraham and the blessing God gave him, and that we too are blessed by the same blessing from God because He considers us descendants of Abraham. Acts 3:25 says, *"And you are heirs of the prophets and of the covenant God made with your fathers. He said to Abraham, 'Through your offspring all peoples on earth will be blessed."* (Acts 3:25)

Romans 4:16 says, *"Therefore, the promise comes by faith, so that it may be by grace and may be guaranteed to all Abraham's offspring—not only to those who are of the law but also to those who have the faith of Abraham. He is the father of us all."*

I have written about the Abrahamic blessing because it is for everyone and also because it shows the importance God places on families and the blessing that comes through being part of God's family.

In summary, the Abrahamic blessing is that God will always be with you, that He will bless those who bless you and curse those who curse you. He will increase your numbers and give you land, and His blessing will pass down to your children. He will bless you and you will be a blessing and He will make your name great. This applies to everyone and shows the blessings of being part of a family, and even more so the blessings of being part of God's family.

Letter

My dear child,

As I was with Abraham, so I am with you. I have given you a new identity as my beloved child. I will never leave you or forsake you. You are no longer an orphan. You are my join heir with Christ. Hold your head up high. I give you double honour for your shame. My glory shines on you. I give you a heritage and you will leave a legacy for your children and your children's children. You are not a pauper. You are royalty. You are a prince or princess. Every blessing I gave Abraham is yours. Seek out and note the blessings and make them your own. Write them out and declare them. I say to you as I did Abraham. Those who bless you I will bless and those who curse you will be cursed. Ask of me what it means for you to receive Abraham's blessings and I will tell you. I will fight for you and together we will be victorious. Do not fear. Nothing is impossible for me. I will contend with those who contend with you. I bless you in every area of life so you will truly live an abundant life. I love you.

Love, your Dad, Almighty God

Here is a list of the many blessings of being part of God's family

- Friendship
- Love
- Belonging
- Sharing
- Being cared for
- Protection
- Welcome
- Doing life together
- Culture of honour
- Learning from each other
- God's wisdom
- Knowing God's heart
- Spiritual gifts
- Fruit of the Holy Spirit
- A good future
- Healing
- Prophesy

- Angelic protection
- Stops loneliness
- Being known for who you are
- Calling out the gold in people
- Lots of different talents
- A place of blessing
- Place of unity
- Enjoying differences
- Inheritance
- All of God's provision and riches
- Living in God's favour
- A common purpose and destiny
- Reaching others who don't know God
- Knowing your true identity
- Being royalty
- Seeing yourself as God sees you, hope or great expectations
- We only see part of the picture, the rest of the family provide the other part

We have not gone into detail on these blessings above. You may think of others. You may like to pause and see if there is anything that you can recognise and be thankful for.

Families were God's idea, and they are meant to be a blessing. Both our natural family and God's family are meant to be a blessing.

One of the biggest problems in our nation at the moment is loneliness, and we are told in Psalm 68:6 *"God sets the lonely in families."* This is a blessing. In God's family there are so many people that it should be impossible for you to be lonely! This is such a blessing. Wherever you go, there will be people who belong to God's family.

We will all have had experiences of being part of earthly families and some of us may have experienced being part of the church. These experiences influence the way we view what it would be like to be part of God's family. Perhaps you can think how that has affected how you feel about having God as your Father and being part of His family. We need to remember it isn't just people who go to church who are part of God's family.

Blessings of having God as Father

In John 14:6 Jesus says, *"I am the way the truth and the life. No one comes to the father except through me."* I often say, if there is a way there has to be a destination. So, in this verse Jesus says He is the way but what is the destination? It is God the Father. In the Bible it all comes back to God the Father and being in relationship with Him, so let's do an individual exercise to see how you view God as Father and being part of God's family. Please do not write what are the "right" answers but be honest with yourself how you really feel and think. Picture yourself with your hand in Jesus' hand standing on a garden path just inside the garden gate. Ahead of you is the Father's house. What does it look like? Describe in as much detail as you can. You arrive at the door. Is it open or closed? Where is God the Father? If the door is closed, ring the doorbell. Before you ring the bell, how do you feel? How do you think God feels about seeing you? The door opens. Who does the Father greet first? What does He look like? How does He greet Jesus? How does He greet you? What does the Father say, if anything? Do you go inside the house and, if so, what does it look like? How does it feel?

God gave us our imaginations and, if we have given our imaginations to God, it can show us how we are feeling. Having been given to God, our imaginations are sanctified. Look back over what you wrote and if it was negative take time to talk it over with God and give Him your negative emotions. Then ask Him to show you what He is really like as Father and what His house is really like. You now have a picture of how you see God as Father and why. As God is the perfect Father, and also outside of time, He can fulfil all the areas of your life that lack a father's love and care. So, if for instance you have realised that your father was not always there for you, you need to know that God the Father is always there for you and will in fact never leave you. Psalm 139:17-18 AMP *"How precious also are Your thoughts to me, O God! How vast is the sum of them! If I could count them, they would outnumber the sand. When I awake, I am still with You."* In fact Psalm 139 is good to read regularly to be reminded how precious you are to God and how much He loves you. Having God as your Father is a blessing because He loves you and will never leave you. is always there for you which is a blessing.

If you have not been parented well it may be more difficult to think of God as a loving parent, but with God's help you will be able to. Also, you may have had negative experiences with people within church and not think of it as family, but for now we will look at God's design for family and all the blessings that should be present in being part of God's family. I would like you to put aside your previous experience of family and come to see the blessings of God's family with an open heart. In fact, even better, come with great expectation which is the same as hope. Expectations determine what you see, hear and experience, both in the spirit and in the natural. Hope is often seen as wishy washy, but it is a determining force. Hope has to be based on something solid and reliable, and our hope as God's children is based in God. Psalm 146:5, *"Blessed are those whose help is in the Lord the God of Jacob, whose hope is in the Lord their God."*

In fact, God promises to give us hope. Jeremiah 29:11, *"For I know the plans I have for you"* declares the Lord, *"plans to prosper you and not to harm you, plans to give you hope and a future."* Lamentations 3:25 says *"The Lord is good to those whose hope is in him, to the one who seeks him."* The Holy Spirit also helps us to hope. *"May the God of hope fill you with all joy and peace as you trust in him, so that you may overflow with hope by the power of the Holy Spirit."* (Romans 15:13). We are told that love always hopes 1 Corinthians 13:7, *"It always protects, always trusts, always hopes, always perseveres."* Ephesians 1:18 says, *"I pray that the eyes of your heart may be enlightened in order* that you may know the hope to which he has called you, the riches of his glorious inheritance in his holy people." 1 Timothy 6:17 says "Command those who are rich in this present world not to be arrogant or to put their hope in wealth, which is so uncertain, but to put their hope in God who richly provides us with everything for our enjoyment."

The biggest blessing is to be God's child and have God as your Father. 1 John 3:1 says, "See what great love the father has lavished on us, that we should be called children of God! And that is what we are!" It is important and a blessing to know who our parents are, as this helps us to know who we are and gives us our identity and sense of worth.

Blessing of the mother heart of God

God is not just our Father. He mothers us as well. The Holy Spirit shows us the mother heart of God. From the very beginning, the Holy Spirit is described as hovering or brooding over the waters which is a way that mother animals are described. The Holy Spirit is known as the comforter which is also a way a mother's love is shown, in comfort.

Knowing the comforting love of God is a blessing.

In Genesis 1:27 it says, "So God created man in his own image, in the image of God he created them; male and female he created them." God isn't human but He is described as love. Love can be shown in masculine and feminine, maternal, and paternal ways. So, God has both a mothering and fathering love that is shown in the Bible but also in the ways God shows His love to us. A mother's love is thought to be shown in compassion and in Isaiah 49:15 it says of God, "Can a mother forget the baby at her breast and have no compassion on the child she has born? Though she may forget, I will not forget you!" This verse shows that it seems inconceivable that mothers are not compassionate to their children, but God is even more compassionate. This verse also shows God never forgets you or abandons you and this is a blessing. In Exodus 22:27 God says, "When they cry out to me, I will hear, for I am compassionate." Again, in Exodus 34:6 it says, *"And he passed in front of Moses, proclaiming, 'The Lord, the Lord, the compassionate and gracious God, slow to anger, abounding in love and faithfulness.'"* Several times in the New Testament we are told that Jesus had compassion on the crowds. For example, in Matthew 14:14, *"When Jesus landed and saw a large crowd, he had compassion on them and healed their sick."* Compassion will always evoke a response and require an action. Knowing and experiencing God's compassion for you is a blessing.

Being a son and daughter

Our relationship with God our Father will be influenced with how our relationship with our earthly parents was or is. So how was or is your relationship with your parents? Spend a few minutes thinking about this and writing down your thoughts. If this is painful for you, turn to God and He will help you and comfort you in this situation. He is not unaware or distant. He is aware of all our circumstances and our history. Furthermore, He is able to bring hope to the most desperate situations.

Think about how you were parented.

Were your parents strict, lenient, easy going, stern, demonstrative, cold, encouraging, discouraging, inclusive, having unspoken expectations? You can add any further descriptions. Be as full in your description as you can be. Then think how you were as a son or daughter to your parents, both as a child and as an adult. Describe as fully as possible. Did you honour your parents? Did you respect them and listen to their advice and thoughts? Did you care for them as they got older? Did you help them? Did you visit them? What did you think about them? Were you demonstrative? Were you open with them? Did you hide things from them? Did you talk things through? Did you obey them? Did you disregard them? Did you love them? Do you think they felt loved by you? Did you spend time with them? If they are dead now, how do you think of them? Do you honour their memory? These questions are not to make you feel guilty but to show you how you were with your earthly parents can be carried over to how you are with God as your Father. Being God's child is one of the greatest blessings you can have, but this can be spoilt if you haven't learnt how to be a son or daughter. Being a son or daughter is a heart attitude and means you need to be a son or daughter from your heart and then the right actions will follow. This is a blessing because it means you can give God any negative feelings and He will exchange them for positive feelings. It is not about how your parents behave; it is about how you respond. It is about honouring your parents, which is the first command with a promise. Exodus 20:12, *Honour your father and mother, so that you may live long in the land your God is giving you."* This is yet another blessing, that of long life.

From before the beginning of creation God's desire was to have children made in His image that He would parent perfectly so that they would grow into completely secure adults who knew that they were loved, wanted, cherished and that they had a purpose. They would know who they were and what they were worth and would know their purpose in life. They would live in a perfect loving relationship with Him as their Father. They would know Him and His heart and would walk in unison with Him, co-labouring with Him to look after the world. I am sure you can see that being a son or daughter to God in this type of relationship would be a blessing.

God so wants to parent us as we are told in Jeremiah 3:19, *"I myself said, 'How gladly would I treat you like my children and give you a pleasant land the most beautiful inheritance of any nation.' I thought you would call me 'Father' and not turn away from following me."* He has good plans for your future. So, are you willing to be a son or daughter of God? You have seen what a good Father God is and how much He loves you and wants to parent you. Are you a good son or daughter to God? Do you know Him as your Father? One of my sayings is, you do not know what you do not know until you know you know you do not know it. In this case you might not have known you could have a real living father/child relationship with God and so you have done nothing about it. Now you know you can have that father/child relationship, do you want it? If you already know God as your Dad, how would you like to be a better son or daughter to God? Are you a mature or an immature child? Is the father/child relationship with God the most important one to you in your life? Are you aware of the blessings of being God's child?

One of the blessings of being God's child is that God promises if we ask, we will receive. Matthew 7:7-8 says, *"Ask and it will be given to you; seek and you will find; knock and the door will be opened to you. For everyone who asks receives; the one who seeks finds; and to the one who knocks, the door will be opened."* Then in verse 11, *"If you then, though you are evil, know how to give good gifts to your children, how much more will your father in heaven give good gifts to those who ask him!"*

God loves to give good gifts, as seen in the verse above but also in James 1:17 GNB, *"Every good gift and every perfect present comes from heaven; it comes down from God, the father of the heavenly lights, who does not change or cause darkness by turning."* As our heavenly Father is like this, we can talk to Him freely, asking for what we need and want. This is a blessing of being God's son or daughter. This changes the way we pray; the reason that we're answered is that the Father loves giving good gifts to His children. It is no longer a ritual but a relationship. God the Father answers us because He loves us and wants to take care of us and provide for us. This is a blessing of being God's son or daughter.

Prayer to receive the Father's love (for those who have struggles with parents)

Father I come to you with the pain of the past, any pain in the present.
I ask that you would bring your healing and hope where I have wounds and despair.

I ask that you would give me your perspective of how much I am loved by you.
That you will give me a revelation of the Father's love.
That will never leave nor forsake.
That will never harm or hurt.
That is constant and true.
That wants the best for me.
That is there to encourage and bless.
That is faithful and sure.
May I rest in your love.
May I discover joy in your presence.
May you restore what I have lost.
And give me abundant life.
May you work in the ongoing challenges I face.
Guide me and help me in the relationships I struggle with.
Give me your wisdom and work in them to bring change.
I ask all these things
In and through the name of Jesus,

Amen.

You may find that it would be helpful to say this prayer as many times as you need to.

I am sure that some may have had a more positive experience with their parents and so here is a prayer for you.

Prayer to receive the Father's love

Father thank you for my parents and all the love that they showed me.
Help me to see where they gave me a true reflection of you and your love.
Please help me to know your love more and more.
Please help me to accept you as my Father and realise I am not letting my earthly parents down by loving you as my Dad.
Please help me to get over any regrets I have in the way I treated my parents and give those regrets to you.

Thank you that they understood me even when I did not realise.

Thank you for their example and all their wisdom and advice.

Thank you for all the memories I have of them.

Where there are any painful memories, please give me your comfort.

Let your grace cover any mistakes or things that were lacking in my childhood.

Thank you that I have a new life with you as my Father.

Please help me grow in this relationship and show me what it means to be a son or daughter to you.

Amen.

You may be wondering why you have been asked to think on your own parent relationships. It is because until you can be a son or daughter from the heart to your earthly parents it is difficult to be a son or daughter to your Heavenly Father. You have to first recognise where you are, before you can move to where God wants you to be. There is no case so bad that God can't bring healing, forgiveness, and a way of moving on, even if that means you can't meet with the parents because for health and safety reasons. We have asked you to pray the prayers above so that you can move forward to being a good son or daughter and live in the blessings of being God's child.

There are more blessings of being God's son or daughter and maybe you would like to search out what they are.

Blessing of brothers and sisters

In your earthly family brothers and sisters are constant companions. They are there through your everyday life. If you are bored, you have someone to talk to and play with. Likewise, as part of God's family those who are God's children are your brother and sisters and you can do everyday life with them. As you become friends with them and get to know them, they are there for you and you can talk together and relax and enjoy daily life with each other. This is the blessing of brothers and sisters.

Likewise, brothers and sisters are there for you to discuss your plans and feelings. If you have more than one brother or sister you talk to, you can get a variety of opinions and see which things are agreed on most. This is a blessing.

Brothers and sisters understand the family way of life better than anyone outside the family does and can help you sort out family relationships and the best way to approach your parents about things. This is a blessing.

There are more blessings to being and having brothers and sisters and perhaps you would like to think of them all. One of the biggest of being a brother or sister in God's family is that wherever you go there will be brothers and sisters for you to meet. You need never be lonely or not have someone to speak to.

Spiritual mums and dads

There are blessings to being a spiritual mum or dad and blessings to having a spiritual mum and dad. You may not have every thought about this before, even if there are people in your life that may well be spiritual mums and dads to you. God blesses us with people who look out for us and are committed to our spiritual growth.

Although spiritual mums and dads have been around since Bible times it has only been in recent years that they have been recognised and appreciated. God the Father is the main parenting figure we should have, but He uses others in His family, the church, to be a spiritual parent to us. It is a special relationship and a blessing, but should never take the place of us being God's child and having God as our Father.

I believe having a spiritual mum and dad or being a spiritual mum or dad is part of the fulfilment of Malachi 4:5-6 NKJV, *"Behold I will send Elijah the prophet before the coming of the great and dreadful day of the Lord. And he will turn the hearts of the fathers to the children, and the hearts of the children to their fathers."* This is a mutual turning of hearts towards each other and honouring and valuing each other. It is both generations in the parent/child relationship who have turned their hearts toward each other. This is a blessing.

Having talked of this being a newly recognised thing in church, we read about it in scripture. 1 Timothy 5:1-2 NLT says, *"Never speak harshly to an older man but appeal to him respectfully as you would to your own father. Talk to younger men as you would to your own brothers. Treat older women as you would your mother, and treat younger women with all purity as you would your own sisters."* Paul also describes such relationships in 1 Thessalonians 2:7 AMP, *"But we behaved gently when we were among you, like a devoted mother tenderly caring for her own children"* or the

The Message version describes this in more detail: *"Even though we had some standing as Christ's apostles we never threw our weight around or tried to come across as important with you or anyone else. We weren't aloof with you. We took you just as you were. We were never patronising, never condescending, but we cared for you the way a mother cares for her children. We loved you dearly. Not content to just pass on the message we wanted to give you our hearts. And we did."* Having a spiritual mum or dad who treats you in this way is a blessing.

Spiritual mums and dads are a great blessing and can speak into your life in a way other people cannot. Their prayers seem to have more effect and you can receive a spiritual inheritance from them as well as a father's blessing. A father's blessing can be prayed by a man or woman, as it is hearing God the Father's heart for that person and praying that over them. In Bible times a father's blessing was seen as essential, as shown by Jacob stealing Esau's blessing. You can read about this in Genesis 27. A father's blessing bestows security, identity, a sense of worth, of being loved, of having a purpose and a sense of belonging.

The inheritance you receive is a blessing, as you benefit from their spiritual wisdom, experience, and anointing.

Being a spiritual mum or dad is an attitude of heart rather than a role or title. It is normally the recipient who says they see you as a spiritual mum or dad in my experience. This is a privilege and a blessing.

As well as being a spiritual mum myself I have spiritual mums and dads. When I asked them if they would be a spiritual mum or dad to me, it was because I had heard God say to me that He was giving those people to me as a spiritual mum or dad. They agreed, and the relationship has grown over the years. These people are a great blessing to me, and I love and respect them. These relationships are part of the blessing of belonging to God's family. People have the choice of whether they are a spiritual mum or dad or not. Our heavenly Father is always there and will provide you with people to care for you.

You do not normally have many spiritual mums and dads and in 1 Corinthians 4:15 it says, *"Even if you had ten thousand guardians in Christ you do not have many fathers, for in Christ Jesus I became your father through the gospel."* You may like to read this chapter in full. This chapter shows that rather than being a teacher or preacher or mentor, a spiritual mum or dad loves you like their child and all they do or say is out of love. However, they are not trying to point you to themselves, but rather point you to your Heavenly Father, God. This is a blessing and comes from being part of God's family.

Spiritual mums and dads are such a blessing so, do you have a spiritual mum or dad? If not, you may like to spend time asking God to give you a spiritual mum and dad. You can ask Him who these people should be. Once you know who they are, you can then ask them if they would be a spiritual mum or dad to you and say you believe God has pointed them out to you. As already mentioned, they have a choice as to whether they would like to do this or not. God will bless you with those who love and care for you.

Being a spiritual mum or dad is also a blessing. It is a unique relationship. You disciple the people God gives you but, more than that, you come alongside them as you would your own children and it is as if they become an extended part of your family. You love them as a parent would and pray for and bless them regularly.

Are you a spiritual mum or dad to anyone? If not, ask God who He is giving you to be a spiritual mum or dad to.

You can also be a spiritual mum or dad to a nation or nations. You may have this role prophesied over you and find that without any effort on your part you have a heart for a particular nation or nations and minister at a national level. This has happened to me and was something that happened naturally or maybe I should say supernaturally. The Bible talks of this and for instance Romans 4:17 says: *"As it is written: 'I have made you a father of many nations'"*

Spiritual grandparents

I had not heard the term spiritual grandparents until a few years ago and it was in my home church that I first heard it used in relation to an older couple in our church. Somehow it sparked something in me, and I knew that it was a spiritual thing, ordained by God. Since then, I have heard spiritual grandparents being talked about more widely. God himself is a trigenerational God, as He introduces himself as 'I am the God of Abraham, Isaac, and Jacob'. That is, God in relationship through three generations of a family. In fact, God introduces himself this way four times. This is in Exodus 3:6, Matthew 22:32, Mark 12:26 and Acts 7:32. These all refer to when God talked to Moses from the burning bush.

In the natural, you can be a grandparent and a parent simultaneously and that is true of spiritual grandparents as well. Having grandparents, both spiritual and in the natural, is a great blessing.

Grandparents are a source of wisdom and advice and give a sense of history through tales of their childhood. These are a blessing. Their words are valued because of their experience. I have been blessed during my life by having relationships with Christians who would have been my grandparents' age and had been Christians since their youth. We studied the Bible together and they shared truths they had learnt through the years and good ways to live as a Christian, and would also pray for me and give me advice. I consider that a real blessing though most of these people have now died. However, it has nothing to do with physical age but more the length of their walk with God and experience as to whether someone is seen as a spiritual grandparent.

Grandparents are mentioned in the Bible. For example, 2 Timothy 1:5 AMP says, *"I remember your sincere and unqualified faith [the surrendering of your entire self to God in Christ with confident trust in His power, wisdom, and goodness, a faith] which first lived in [the heart of] your grandmother Lois and your mother Eunice, and I am confident that it is in you as well."* We can see from this verse that his natural grandmother was also his spiritual grandmother and passed her faith onto her child and then to her grandson.

The word grandfather only occurs in 2 Samuel (2 Samuel 9:7; 2 Samuel 16:3; and 2 Samuel 19:20). These refer to Saul's grandson, the son of Jonathan, whose name is Mephibosheth. Elsewhere, it is mentioned after someone's name, i.e., the son of.... or the grandson of....

In Biblical times who you were linked to for at least three generations back was very important. Your lineage gave credit to you in your standing in the community, as grandparents were seen to give you wisdom faith and truth. This is a blessing of being part of God's family and having spiritual grandparents. People took note of who your parents and grandparents were. Today Christians take note of who your spiritual parents and grandparents are.

God also takes note of His promises to your parents and grandparents and says things such as in Joshua 1:5, *"As I was with Moses, so I will be with you"*. In this case Joshua was Moses' spiritual son and successor. Still, God honoured His promises to Moses in Joshua's life. In Genesis 35:12 God says to Jacob, *"The land I gave to Abraham, and Isaac I also give to you, and I will give this land to your descendants after you."* This verse shows how God values the family generational line and grandchildren receive an inheritance from God because of their lineage. A spiritual inheritance passes down from your spiritual grandparents. This is a blessing of being part of God's family.

I have heard it said that parents represent the law and grandparents represent grace. Spiritual parents and grandparents should always speak and act from the heart of God's Father's heart and therefore in love. They are standing in the gap and saying and doing what God is saying and doing. This is another blessing of being part of God's family.

Spiritual grandparents are often older in years but definitely older and more mature spiritually. They will have walked with God many years and had much experience with God they can pass on. They will have experienced spiritual growth and have a deeper level of intercession and relationship with God. Within a church or ministry, they will be widely recognised as having wisdom and revelation and authority from God. This is a blessing. They will probably oversee many, not just an individual. They are likely to be exhibiting the fruit of the Spirit because of their relationship with God over many years. They should be able to share the blessing of God's goodness manifested over their lifetime. They will be able to share their testimony and encourage and mentor younger generations.

Here are some blessings about family.

Blessing for a family

Be blessed...

    ...by being part of a family.
    ...with good relationships with everyone.
    ...by each family member loving each other.
    ...by a common goal within the family.
    ...by making good memories between you.
    ...by good provision for everyone.
    ...by a warm, welcoming family home.
    ...with understanding each other.
    ...by good communication with everyone in the family.

...to forgive each other quickly.

...by saying sorry if you wrong one another.

...to care for each other.

...to share your lives together.

...to be accepted for who you are.

...to appreciate each other.

...to cheer each other on.

...to support each other.

...to celebrate each other.

...to protect each other.

...to speak well of each other.

...to have God at the head of your family.

Blessing of being part of God's family

Be blessed...

...to have God as your Father.

...to have Jesus as your big brother.

...to have brothers and sisters all over the world.

...to be part of God's family locally.

...to be loved by so many people.

...to have a spiritual mum and dad.

...to have people who know you.

...to have people who you know.

...to be a brother or sister to them.

...to have God as a Father in common.

...to love each other.

...to care for each other.

...to all have a common goal.

...to share with each other.

...to hear God together.

...to worship God together.

...to meet together.

...to know God doesn't have favourites.

...God loves each of you as much as Jesus.

...to inherit all God has.

...to bring heaven to earth together.

...to learn from each other as God directs.

...to speak well of each other.

...to do life together.

...to live in abundant life.

Blessing for mothers

Be blessed...

...to be parented by God.

...by knowing your child is a gift from God.

...by being a mum.

...with a healthy loving relationship with your child.

...by supportive relationships.

...by being nurtured by God.

...by nurturing your child.

...with loving relationships.

...to have enough to live and give.

...to feel fulfilled as a mother.

...with good living conditions.

...by spending time with your child.

...with contentment.

...with safety and security.

...with wisdom for dealing with your child.

...with a supportive husband.

...with someone who mothers you.

...with a loving healthy relationship with your husband.

...to parent well.

...with God restoring broken relationships.

...with new beginnings.

...with God's grace covering any mistakes that have been made.

...with hope, patience, and resolve.

...to write new chapters.

...with time with your husband.

...to be appreciated.

...to know you are loved by God and others.

Blessing for grandparents

Be blessed...

>...with knowing all children are a gift from God.
>...with relaxing times spent with your grandchildren.
>...with time spent with your children.
>...with time spent together as a couple.
>...to enjoy the unique relationship of grandparents with
>...their grandchildren.
>...with times of rest and relaxation.
>...to share your wisdom.
>...to be there and listen.
>...to encourage your child and grandchild.
>...to support your child and their role as a parent.
>...when to speak and when to be quiet.
>...with loving relationships within the family.
>...to have fun with your child and grandchild.
>...to be creative.
>...to share interests.
>...with patience.
>...to be appreciated.
>...by being good grandparents.
>...by loving and being loved.
>...by seeing the gold in your child and grandchild.
>...by using your life's experience.
>...by God guiding you in your relationship with your child and grandchild.
>...by knowing God's love for you and your family.

Blessing for fathers

Be blessed...

>...to be a father.
>...to imitate God the Father.
>...to love your child.
>...for your child to love you.
>...to love your child's mother and be loved by her.
>...to know God heals where relationships are difficult.

...to know reconciliation where needed.

...to know God restores the years the locusts have eaten.

...to know God is with you and wants the best for you and your family.

...to parent well.

...to enjoy time with your child and your child enjoy being with you.

...to discipline your child in fairness and love.

...to provide boundaries for your child.

...to spend time with your child.

...to give your child stability.

...to give your child security.

...to provide for your child's needs.

...to be parented by God.

...for God to be your example of a good father.

...with time for yourself.

...with time with your wife.

...to be appreciated.

...to be the best dad you can be.

Going deeper

- How do you feel about being part of God's family?
- Do you recognise the many blessings that we have mentioned about being in God's family?
- How can you improve your relationship within God's family?

Letter

My daughter,

I say my because you are mine. You are my child. You are precious. You are loved. You are part of the beloved. You are included in my family. You have a place at the table. You have a room in my house. When someone is precious, they are valued. They are esteemed. They are recognised. They are included. They are visible. They are delighted in. Now put 'you' instead of 'they'. You are valued. You are esteemed. You are recognised. You are included. You are visible. I watch over you. You are my delight. Where others have spoken other words over you, I speak another word. You are precious.

Your Dad xxx

Prayer

Heavenly Father,
Thank you for the blessing of being adopted in your family. Thank you for everyone else that is in your family. Thank you for all the many blessings that we have written about that come from being in your family. We are so grateful to be your child. We love you. Amen

Blessing

Be blessed by being part of God's family.

Songs

One shall tell another (The wine of the kingdom) by Graham Kendrick (1981)

Books

Finishing Well – A God's-eye view on ageing by Ian Knox (2020)
Walking with God as Father by Wendy Thomas (2013)

Chapter 8

Blessings for various places and people

As you read the blessings in this chapter there may be things that stand out to you that you would like to pray into afterwards on your own or with others. You may like to note the words that particularly speak to you and take them to the Lord in prayer. Write them down if this helps. You may find some things jar because it is not how it is in present day reality. Blessing states things as God would like them to be, not as they necessarily are.

When we bless the nation, we bless ourselves too. If we bless our nation with unity, then we will be blessed when we are living in unity. When we bless our streets then we will enjoy all the blessings from this. Every one of the blessings in this chapter will have a personal connect with us in some way and we will be blessed as a consequence. So, as you bless be aware of this.

We can also bless and travail. We can experience both blessing and sorrow. Blessing is not always a happy feeling. We can seek God about the things that are on our heart. We can even lament. We can bring our complaint before God. So many of the Psalms in the Bible are a lament. There is always a point when you lament where there is the blessing of a declaration of faith that changes everything.

Life gives us both sorrow and joy. And even as we are lamenting God is with us and, as we are told in Romans 8:28, *"we know that in all things God works for the good of those who love him, who have been called according to his purpose."* God is a good Father and wants to bless us in all situations.

Let us now look at some specific blessings you can say of places, people and to celebrate occasions. There is a scripture for each blessing to help you bless. When we speak a blessing, we speak it from the heart, and we have faith it will come to pass.

Nation

There are over 600 references to nation or nations in the Bible. Where we live is the place where we have authority. Yet we can also have a heart and passion to pray for other places and nations. Psalm 2:8 says, *"Ask me, and I will make the nations your inheritance, the ends of the earth your possession."*

Psalm 33:12 ESV – Father we bring you the nation of... *"Blessed is the nation whose God is the Lord, the people whom he has chosen as his heritage!"*

Be blessed...

...to have God at the centre,
...to fulfil your destiny.
...to recognise your Godly heritage.
...to walk in your gifting.
...to be united.
...to be upright and true.
...to value everyone.
...to welcome those who are sent to you.
...to care for the poor.
...to be law abiding.
...to respect those in authority.
...to make good decisions.
...to consider all.
...to be fair.
...to live righteously.
...to be one nation under God.
...to have good relationships with other nations.
...to have safe borders.
...to live at peace.
...across all generations.
...to know your boundaries.
...with a good education for all.
...to celebrate creativity.
...to advance science.
...to work together for the common good.

...whether urban or rural.

...whether coast or inland.

...whether city, town, or village.

...to have all you need.

...with fruit and harvest.

...with industry and enterprise.

...with good government local and national.

...to prosper.

Cities

"You will be blessed in the city, and you will be blessed in the field." (Deuteronomy 28:3 AMP)

Be blessed...

...by being a large community.

...to pool your resources.

...to share your facilities.

...with good facilities.

...with green open spaces.

...with places to relax.

...to consist of communities that stick together.

...for people to feel they belong.

...to welcome and include everyone.

...with caring neighbourhoods.

...to have communities that support each other.

...to get to know your neighbours.

...to enjoy different cultures.

...to learn from each other.

...with safety on the streets.

...with opening yourself to others.

...with strong loving families.

...with unity among the churches.

...with many community activities and opportunities.

...with good schools that provide an excellent education for all.

...to be a city of culture.

...to appreciate your Godly heritage.

...to learn from history.
...with fairness and justice for all.
...with good services.
...with work opportunities.
...with thriving ethical businesses.
...with new enterprises.
...to sustain long standing businesses.
...to be a shining light.
...to be held as a good example.
...with creative solutions to problems.
...to be somewhere people want to live.
...to be a place that tourists want to visit.
...with a sense of purpose and identity.
...that citizens have a sense of pride in the city.

Town

*"And the angel said to him, "Behold, I grant you this request also; I will not destroy this town of which you have spoken." * (Genesis 19:21 AMP)

Father we bring to you the town of.......
.......be blessed by having God at the centre.

Be blessed...

...by good leadership.
...by neighbourhoods working well together.
...by a vision for the town.
...by being a safe place to live.
...to have a good reputation in that nation.
...to thrive.
...to celebrate young and old.
...with intergenerational relationships.
...to care for those who are vulnerable.
...to be a place where people can relax and enjoy themselves.
...by green and open spaces.
...to have excellent facilities.
...with schools that give a good education for all.

...with servant hearted councillors.

...with men and women who lead with integrity.

...with solutions to difficult problems.

...with local services that support the community.

...with unity amongst the churches.

...to see transformation in the town.

...with businesses prospering.

...with provision.

...with enough housing for everyone.

...with loving care homes for the elderly and vulnerable.

...with charities that meet the needs of the town's residents.

...with law and order.

...with good health care.

...with an efficient fire service.

Coast

"The sea is His, for He made it [by His command]; And His hands formed the dry land." (Psalm 95:5 AMP)

Be blessed...

...by the beauty of the coast.

...to praise God for it.

...to be in wonder and in awe at God's creation.

...by wild seas.

...by calm waters.

...by sandy shores.

...by rocks and pebbles.

...by fish that swim in the sea.

...by every living creature in the sea and shore.

...by rockpools to explore.

...by sand to build sandcastles.

...by swimming in the sea.

...by water sports.

...by seashells to collect.

...by the calming effect of the sea.

...by living by the sea.

...whether village, town, or city by the sea.

...with good community.

...to welcome visitors.

...by visitors being considerate.

...to build up relationships with visitors.

...with income from tourism.

...with innovation to support the local economy.

...to care for those who live and work on the sea.

...to have lifeboats that can be used if necessary.

...with volunteers to run them.

...with lifeguards on beaches.

...with good facilities.

...with fresh sea breezes.

...with the sound of seagulls.

...with views of the sea to enjoy.

...with the vastness of the sea.

...with sunsets and sunrises on the horizon.

Blessing for streets

"And your ancient ruins shall be rebuilt; you shall raise up the foundations of many generations; you shall be called the repairer of the breach, the restorer of streets to dwell in." (Isaiah 58:12 RSV)

Be blessed...

...to flourish where you live.

...to have a heart for your street.

...to bring your street to God.

...with good memories.

...with inter-generational relationships on your street.

...to live in harmony.

...with good connections and conversations.

...to bridge divides.

...to love your enemy.

...with safety and security.

...with God's love that casts out all fear.

...by deliverance from all evil.

...with reconciliation where there has been misunderstanding.

...to forgive.

...to look out for each other.

...to care for those you live amongst.

...to look out for their best interests.

...to meet each other's needs.

...to come up with creative solutions to difficult issues.

...to see transformation where needed.

...to have a street with a good reputation.

...for the street to be a desirable place to live.

...to share food together.

...to have fun together.

...to share your lives.

Blessing for estates

"By wisdom a house is built, and through understanding it is established; through knowledge its rooms are filled with rare and beautiful treasures." (Proverbs 24:3-4)

Be blessed...

...to know God as a good Father.

...to receive and experience God the Father's love for you.

...to understand how God the Father sees you.

...to know who you are.

...by being accepted as you are.

...with good relationships.

...to know how loved you are.

...to be valued.

...to be considerate to each other.

...to not judge and not be judged.

...with good neighbours.

...with friends within the estate.

...with a good community.

...with a caring family.

...to support each other.

...to enjoy good times together.
...with a sense of purpose.
...with hope.
...with wellbeing.
...to see good plans fulfilled.
...to prosper.
...with enough to live and to give.
...with good amenities and services.
...with recreation.
...with creativity.
...to use your gifts.
...with green spaces in the estate.
...with a good reputation.
...with those outside the estate supporting you.
...to live in safety and security.
...to have life in abundance.

Blessing for London

"But seek the welfare of the city where I have sent you into exile, and pray to the Lord on its behalf, for in its welfare you will find your welfare." (Jeremiah 29:7 ESV)

Be blessed...

...by being the nation's capital city.
...to lead the way.
...to unite the nation under God.
...to know you are in God's hands.
...to walk in God's authority.
...to be highlighted to the world.
...to be a Godly example.
...to know God.
...to be the seat of parliament.
...to rule in righteousness and truth.
...to be a city of peace.
...to be a city of refuge and security and safety.
...for your streets to be safe.
...to prosper.

...with good services.
...with good amenities.
...with open green spaces.
...with flourishing businesses.
...they trade fairly.
...by being a community of people.
...by people feeling they belong.
...for people to put down roots.
...with a sense of cohesion.
...to be a centre of culture.
...to welcome people from all over the world.
...to be a world changer.
...by almighty God.
...with a unique identity.
...to be known.
...to grow and flourish.
...to house and serve the monarchy.

Blessing for the land

"if my people who are called by my name will humble themselves and pray and seek my face and turn from their wicked ways, I will hear from heaven and will forgive their sins and restore their land." (2 Chronicles 7:14 NLT)

Be blessed...

...that God thinks you are good.
...to be created by God.
...to be fruitful.
...to be productive.
...to be cared for.
...to be farmed sustainably.
...to be well watered.
...to provide good pasture.
...to be appreciated.
...by mankind taking care of you.
...to last forever.
...to be beautiful.

...to provide shelter.
...to be cleansed.
...to fulfil your purpose.
...to be healed from trauma.
...to thrive.
...to be an inheritance.
...to be a blessing.
...as a gift from God.
...to stand through the generations.
...by God your creator.
...to provide a peaceful place.

Blessing for farmers

"Then Isaac planted [seed] in that land [as a farmer] and reaped in the same year a hundred times [as much as he had planted], and the Lord blessed and favoured him." (Genesis 26:12 AMP)

Be blessed...

...to have fertile land.
...to make the most of what you have.
...to have healthy livestock.
...to be vigilant in your care for them.
...to farm well.
...to receive a fair price for all you sell.
...to be inventive to maximise your yield.
...to have good family relationships.
...with time off.
...to be able to relax.
...to work hard and be productive.
...to enjoy the beauty of the countryside.
...to be satisfied in your work.
...to network with other farmers to share ideas and resources.
...to have good friends.
...to have fun.
...to stay safe.

...to have equipment that is regularly maintained.

...to have workers that work well.

...to have places to share community.

...to face uncertainty knowing God is with you.

...that God is with you in times of trouble.

...with provision when you need it.

...with good health and wellbeing.

...to look out for others wellbeing.

...with gateway support, as necessary.

...with your strength being renewed each day.

...with good sleep.

...to apply the word of God to your life.

...to have peace whatever the situation.

...to enjoy the fruit of your labours.

Village blessing

"These towns and their villages were the inheritance of the Gadites, according to their clans." (Joshua 13:28)

Be blessed...

...to live in beautiful countryside.

...to be surrounded by nature.

...to enjoy local walks.

...to be a close knit community that cares for each other.

...to know your neighbour.

...to look out for their interests.

...to support shops and businesses nearby.

...to buy food from local farmers.

...to have good facilities.

...with schools that educate well.

...with sport provision.

...with libraries that can be enjoyed whatever your age.

...to have excellent transport networks.

...with community hubs to gather people together.

...with local councillors who represent you well.

...with the church at the heart of the community.

...to have fun and relaxation with others you know.

...to have good local healthcare.

...with entrepreneurs to grow the economy.

...to hear the good news.

...to see revival on the land.

Blessing for a person

"For God so loved the world that he gave his one and only Son, that whoever believes in him shall not perish but have eternal life." (John 3:16)

Be blessed...

...to know Jesus as your Saviour.

...to know God the Father as your dad.

...to know the Holy Spirit as a person.

...to know God in all His fulness.

...with good, healthy, life giving relationships.

...with good relationships in your family.

...with all you need to live and give.

...to love and be loved.

...to have a good home and caring neighbours.

...with good health.

...with God's peace and knowing He loves you.

...with God's joy.

...with contentment.

...to be who God made you to be.

...to know your identity.

...by seeing yourself as God sees you.

...to know and fulfil your destiny.

Blessing for neighbours

"'You shall love the Lord your God with all your heart, and with all your soul, and with all your mind, and with all your strength. The second is this, 'You shall love your neighbour as yourself.' There is no other commandments greater than these." (Mark 12:30-31 NRSV)

Be blessed...

...to love your neighbour.

...to get to know your neighbours.

...for your neighbours to get to know you.

...to hear your neighbour's story.

...to share your story.

...to give your love testimony as you have opportunity.

...to offer and receive hospitality.

...to welcome new neighbours.

...to part well with neighbours moving on.

...to give and receive gifts.

...to pray for your neighbour.

...to persevere for the things laid on your heart to pray for them.

...with timely and meaningful conversations.

...to stop and listen.

...to encourage one another.

...to share helpful information.

...to offer practical support.

...by being friends with your neighbours.

...to comfort those who mourn.

...to come together for good.

...to bring colour where it is grey.

...to plant beautiful gardens for others to enjoy.

...to share life together.

Blessing for the Royal Family

"I urge you, first of all, to pray for all people. Ask God to help them; intercede on their behalf, and give thanks for them. Pray this way for kings and all who are in authority so that we can live peaceful and quiet lives marked by godliness and dignity. This is good and pleases God our Saviour, who wants everyone to be saved and to understand the truth." (1 Timothy 2:1-4 NLT)

Be blessed...

...to know God's hand on your life.

...to know God was there when you were born.

...that God is present all through your life.
...to know God's anointing on you.
...to follow God's guidance.
...for God to sustain you.
...to hear about God.
...to come to know Him for yourself.
...to seek God's face.
...to reign in righteousness and truth.
...with Godly advisors.
...with good family relationships.
...to support each other.
...with healing when it hurts.
...to forgive.
...with vision.
...with wisdom.
...with discernment.
...to rule justly.
...to understand all walks of life.
...to love the people.
...to carry responsibility well.
...to live with integrity.
...with good friends and people you can trust.
...to flourish in your giftings.
...to encourage others.
...with times of relaxation.
...with rest.
...to worship God.
...to share your faith.
...to live in unity.
...with the right word in season.
...to honour and be honoured.
...to engage well with all generations.
...with diplomacy.
...to represent the best interests of the nation.
...with good international relationships.
...with protection.
...to unite the country.
...to speak prophetically as the Holy Spirit leads.

...with good relationships with the government.

...to be impartial.

...to be thankful for all the good things you have.

...to use your money wisely.

...to steward what you have.

...to be loved.

Blessing for leaders

"Where there is no [wise, intelligent] guidance, the people fall [and go off course like a ship without a helm], But in the abundance of [wise and godly] counsellors there is victory." (Proverbs 11:14 AMP)

Be blessed...

...to know you are loved.

...to know you are God's child.

...that God has been with you on your journey.

...that you are not alone.

...to know God is for you.

...to know God is with you.

...with wisdom and discernment.

...to be guided by God.

...with good friends.

...with people you can trust and confide in.

...with protection.

...with satisfaction.

...with inspiration.

...with insight.

...as you prepare sermons.

...to encounter God as you do.

...as you speak God's word.

...to see God at work in people's lives.

...to overflow with hope.

...with solutions to difficult problems.

...to know when to speak and when to be silent.

...to be there for others.

...for others to be there for you.

...to navigate stormy waters.

...to exercise Godly authority as appropriate.

...with diplomacy.

...to get on well with other church leaders.

...with church unity across where you live.

...with vision.

...to know your neighbourhood well.

...to know people in your community.

...to see people with God's eyes.

...to value others.

...to care for those in need.

...with good provision.

...with time spent with God.

...with refreshment.

...having time with family and friends.

...to see people come to faith.

...to nurture and disciple believers.

...to be appreciated.

...to have times of fun and relaxation.

...to recognise giftings in others and encourage them.

...to build up a team for God's purposes.

...to receive ministry yourself when needed.

...with comfort when you mourn.

...to comfort others who mourn.

...to celebrate all God is doing.

...with abundant life.

Blessing for churches

"He went through Syria and Cilicia, strengthening the churches." (Acts 15:41)

Be blessed...

...that God loves every person connected with the church.

...that God wants an abundant life for everyone.

...that God has good plans for all in the church.

...that God has a purpose for the church.

...that God will guide the church.

...for all the churches to work together in unity.

...for the church to have a vision for your community.

...to love everyone and see them through God's eyes.

...to have all your needs met by God.

...to be a welcoming community.

...with understanding.

...to know God's plans and see them fulfilled.

...to forgive any that wrong you.

...to live in love.

...to meet other's needs.

...to introduce people to God.

...to disciple each other.

...to experience God's grace and mercy.

...to be a light in your neighbourhood.

...with a well earnt, good reputation.

...to be fair and just to all.

...to have unconditional love at the centre of all your relationships.

...to have God as the head of the church and central to it all.

Blessing of old age based on Psalm 71

Be blessed...

...that God is your secure shelter.

...that He will never let you down.

...that His justice is your breakthrough.

...that He intentionally listens to your quietest whisper.

...He saves you from all your enemies.

...that God is your place of protection.

...to coming back to hide yourself in Him.

...God is your high fortress where you are kept safe.

...to have God's help to escape from cruel and wicked men.

...to be saved from the hands of the evil one.

...to have God as your only hope.

...to hold onto Him trusting Him all your life

...to have God supporting you from the day you were born.

...that God loves you, helping you through life's journey.

...for God to make you into a miracle.

...to trust Him and praise Him because of this.

...to have people to marvel at your success because of God your mighty protector.

...to overflow with praise for all God has done.

...that His splendour thrills you all day long.

...that you are not set aside now you are old.

...that God does not let go of you when your strength is gone.

...that God knows when your enemies are plotting to harm you.

...that God stays close to you and does not just watch from a distance.

...that God hurries to help you.

...that God hears your cries.

...to trust that God will help you.

...to praise God and magnify His glory.

...to know you couldn't begin to count the times God has been there for you.

...to never run out of things to say about God's faithfulness in keeping you from danger.

...to come forth in God's mighty strength.

...to tell everyone that God alone is the perfect one.

...that God has been your teacher from childhood.

...to tell everyone of God's miracle-wonders.

...that now you are old and grey God does not walk away.

...to declare God's ways to the next generation

...with God's mighty miracles and excitement.

...to show others God's magnificent power.

...that God's glorious righteousness reaches to the high heavens.

...that no one can be compared to God.

...that no one is God's equal.

...that God is a God of marvels and wonders.

...that God revives you again when you sink down with trials and troubles.

...for God to give you more greatness than before.

...for God to turn to you and comfort you once again.

...to praise God because of His faithful heart towards you.

...to shout and sing praises to God for all He is to you.

...that God is your Saviour and lover of your soul.

...to never stop telling others how perfect God is.

...for your enemies to slink away ashamed and defeated.

Blessing for young people

"Don't let anyone look down on you because you are young, but set an example for believers in speech, in conduct, in love, in faith and in purity." (1 Timothy 4:12)

Be blessed...

...by knowing you are a gift from God.

...to know God as a good Father.

...with parents who love you.

...by your family.

...by knowing God loves you.

...by knowing God has good plans for your life.

...by family and friends who love you.

...by them wanting the best for you.

...to be safe.

...to not be with others who lead you astray.

...with a sense of purpose and destiny.

...with a good sense of identity.

...by loving yourself.

...to be true to yourself.

...to know you are valued.

...to appreciate all your unique qualities.

...to use your gifts and abilities to help not harm.

...with ambition.

...with a sense of achievement.

...by knowing what your capabilities are.

...to stretch yourself.
...to learn.
...with a good education.
...to succeed.
...to be provided for.
...with good health and plenty of energy.
...with enjoying exercise.
...with good communication.
...with a sense of belonging.
...to be nurtured in your Christian faith.
...to be part of a local church.
...to discover all God has for you.
...to have a sense of adventure.
...with hope for the future.

Blessing for a family

"For this reason I kneel before the Father, from whom every family in heaven and on earth derives its name." (Ephesians 3:14-15)

Be blessed...

...by being part of a family.
...with good relationships with everyone.
...by each family member loving each other.
...by a common goal within the family.
...by making good memories between you.
...by good provision for everyone.
...by a warm, welcoming family home.
...with understanding each other.
...by good communication with everyone in the family.
...to forgive each other quickly.
...by saying sorry if you wrong one another.
...to care for each other.
...to share your lives together.
...to be accepted for who you are.
...to appreciate each other.
...to cheer each other on.

...to support each other.

...to celebrate each other.

...to protect each other.

...to speak well of each other.

...to have God at the head of your family.

Blessing of being part of God's family

"...so that He might redeem and liberate those who were under the Law, that we [who believe] might be adopted as sons [as God's children with all rights as fully grown members of a family]. (Galatians 4:4-5 AMP)

Be blessed...

...to have God as your Father.

...to have Jesus as your big brother.

...to have brothers and sisters all over the world.

...to be part of God's family locally.

...to be loved by so many people.

...to have a spiritual mum and dad.

...to have people who know you.

...to have people who you know.

...to be a brother or sister to them.

...to have God as a Father in common.

...to love each other.

...to care for each other.

...to all have a common goal.

...to share with each other.

...to hear God together.

...to worship God together.

...to meet together.

...to know God does not have favourites.

...that God loves each of you as much as Jesus.

...to inherit all God has.

...to bring heaven to earth together.

...to learn from each other as God directs.

...to speak well of each other.

...to do life together.

...to live in abundant life.

Blessing for mothers

"As one whom his mother comforts, so I will comfort you…"
(Isaiah 66:13)

Be blessed…

...to be parented by God.

...Be blessed by knowing your child is a gift from God.

...Be blessed by being a mum.

...Be blessed with a healthy loving relationship with your child.

...by supportive relationships.

...by being nurtured by God.

...by nurturing your child.

...with loving relationships.

...to have enough to live and give.

...to feel fulfilled as a mother.

...with good living conditions.

...by spending time with your child.

...with contentment.

...with safety and security.

...with wisdom for dealing with your child.

...with a supportive husband.

...with someone who mothers you.

...with a loving healthy relationship with your husband.

...to parent well.

...with God restoring broken relationships.

...with new beginnings.

...with God's grace covering any mistakes that have been made.

...with hope, patience, and resolve.

...to write new chapters.

...with time with your husband.

...to be appreciated.

...to know you are loved by God and others.

Blessing for grandparents

"Grandchildren are the crown of aged men, and the glory of children is their fathers [who live godly lives]." (Proverbs 17:6 AMP)

Be blessed...

> ...with knowing all children are a gift from God.
> ...with relaxing times spent with your grandchildren.
> ...with time spent with your children.
> ...with time spent together as a couple.
> ...to enjoy the unique relationship of grandparents with their grandchildren.
> ...with times of rest and relaxation.
> ...to share your wisdom.
> ...to be there and listen.
> ...to encourage your child and grandchild.
> ...to support your child and their role as a parent.
> ...when to speak and when to be quiet.
> ...with loving relationships within the family.
> ...to have fun with your child and grandchild.
> ...to be creative.
> ...to share interests.
> ...with patience.
> ...to be appreciated.
> ...by being good grandparents.
> ...by loving and being loved.
> ...by seeing the gold in your child and grandchild.
> ...by using your life's experience.
> ...by God guiding you in your relationship with your child and grandchild.
> ...by knowing God's love for you and your family.

Blessing for fathers

"And he will turn the hearts of fathers to their children and the hearts of children to their fathers." (Malachi 4:6 ESV)

Be blessed...

...to be a father.
...to imitate God the Father.
...to love your child.
...for your child to love you.
...to love your child's mother and be loved by her.
...to know God heals where relationships are difficult.
...to know reconciliation where needed.
...to know God restores the years the locusts have eaten.
...to know God is with you and wants the best for you and your family.
...to parent well.
...to enjoy time with your child and your child enjoy being with you.
...to discipline your child in fairness and love.
...to provide boundaries for your child.
...to spend time with your child.
...to give your child stability.
...to give your child security.
...to provide for your child's needs.
...to be parented by God.
...for God to be your example of a good father.
...with time for yourself.
...with time with your wife.
...to be appreciated.
...to be the best dad you can be.

Blessing for children and grandchildren

"Children are a gift from the Lord; they are a reward from him." (Psalm 127:3 NLT)

Be blessed...

...to know you are loved.

...to know you are wanted.

...to know you are unique.

...to know you are full of good things.

...to know God delights in you.

...to know God loves you.

...to have fun.

...to be creative.

...to have good friends.

...with a good education.

...with many opportunities.

...to know God is your Heavenly Father.

...to know the care of others.

...to be safe and secure.

...to know you have a good future.

...to be provided for.

...to be part of a loving family.

...with good relationships.

...with all you need.

...to not worry or be fearful.

...with an abundant life.

Blessing for prodigals

"But while he was still a long way off, his father saw him and felt compassion, and ran and embraced him and kissed him." (Luke 15:20 ESV)

Be blessed...

...to know your heavenly Father loves you.

...to know Father God longs for your return.

...to know God as your heavenly Father.

...to know Father God constantly looks out for you.

...to know how precious you are to God.

...to come to the end of yourself.

...to hit rock bottom.

...to come to your senses.

...to remember how good your Father is.

...to remember life in your Father's house.
...to remember how kind and caring your Father is.
...to repent.
...to return home.
...to receive the Father's embrace.
...by your heavenly Father's forgiveness.
...by your heavenly Father's acceptance of you.
...to be welcomed home.
...to be treated like a son or daughter.
...to have your identity affirmed.
...to be part of God's family.
...by your heavenly Father trusting you.
...by having your heavenly Father's authority.
...by being celebrated.
...with a sense of purpose.
...to be provided for by God.
...with new beginnings.
...to start over with hope.

Broken lives

"He heals the broken-hearted and binds up their wounds."
(Psalm 147:3 ESV)

...Broken lives
...Due to knives.
...People are stabbing.
...Words are jabbing.
...Opening wounds that shouldn't be there.
...Where is the love, where is the care?
...Hatred spreading through the nation.
...Spreading pain in each generation.
...Lives are being wasted.
...Despair is being tasted.
...What do we do?
...To start anew.
...Where is our hope?
...How do we cope?
...God is the answer, and He loves you.

...Turn to Him, He will see you through.

Blessing for those impacted by gun and knife crime

"Do not repay evil with evil or insult with insult. On the contrary, repay evil with blessing, because to this you were called so that you may inherit a blessing." (1 Peter 3:9)

Be blessed...

    ...with a reason to live.
    ...with a sense of purpose.
    ...to know God loves you.
    ...to know God forgives you.
    ...you can start anew.
    ...to know there is hope for you.
    ...to forgive and be forgiven.
    ...with a new way of life.
    ...to love instead of hate.
    ...to be better not bitter.
    ...with a different way of seeing things.
    ...with a better way of sorting differences.
    ...to be welcomed into God's family.
    ...to be accepted.
    ...to be comforted.
    ...with good healthy emotions.
    ...to receive love.
    ...with a sense of belonging.
    ...to be comforted.
    ...with healing of memories.
    ...to sleep well at night.
    ...with solutions.
    ...to give a good example.
    ...with answers.
    ...to come into all your potential.
    ...to flourish.
    ...with a fruitful life.

Birthday blessing

"You saw me before I was born. Every day of my life was recorded in your book. Every moment was laid out before a single day had passed." (Psalm 139:16 NLT)

Be blessed...

...God knitted you together in your mother's womb.

...God saw who He created you to be before you became you.

...God knows everything about you.

...God understands your every thought.

...God is there at your waking and sleeping.

...when you wake each morning God is still with you.

...with another year of life.

...that God has good plans for you.

...that before you had seen the light of day, the number of days God had planned for you were written in His book.

...that God's plans give you a future and a hope.

...God has gone into your future to prepare the way.

...that God loves you.

...that others love you.

...by the wonder of creation.

...with good friends.

...with fun and relaxation.

...that people celebrate you.

...by being God's child.

...that God celebrates you.

...to live a long and happy life.

...with a sense of purpose.

...with enough to live and enough to give.

...with God's peace.

...by God's protection.

...to know God thinks you are worth dying for.

...to see and receive all God's blessings.

...to be grateful for all good things.

...with abundant life.

...God cherishes you constantly.

...God thinks of you every single moment. You are always in His thoughts.

...God places His hand of blessing on your head.

You are blessed...

...to have God as your Father.

...that God is a good Father.

...to be unconditionally loved by God.

...to always have God with you.

...that God loves you as much as His son Jesus.

...that Jesus is your big brother.

...to share Jesus's inheritance.

...that God calls you His child.

...to be part of God's family.

...with numerous brothers and sisters.

...that God constantly thinks of you.

...that God knows the number of hairs on your head.

...that God watches over you.

...that God knitted you together in your mother's womb.

...that God's thoughts of you are more numerous than the

...grains of sand on the seashore.

...that God has good plans for you.

...that God gives you a hope and a future.

...to have everlasting life.

...to be indwelt by God's Holy Spirit.

...to hear God's voice.

...that God will guide you.

...that God forgives you.

...that God provides for you.

...that God protects you.

...that God inspires you.

...that God sees you through His son Jesus.

...that God sees you as Holy and righteous.

...that God gives you His authority.

...that God anoints you.

...with every spiritual blessing.

...that you have an open heaven over you.

...that God draws near to you as you draw near to Him.

...to know God.

...that you are no longer an orphan.

...by God's peace.

...by God's joy.

...with all God has.

...with abundant life.

Blessing for Old People's Homes and Care Homes

"even to your old age I am he, and to grey hairs I will carry you. I have made, and I will bear; I will carry and will save." (Isaiah 46:4 ESV)

Be blessed...

...by enjoying where you live.

...by a sense of belonging.

...to be part of a healthy loving community.

...to have good friendships.

...with staff who are loving and caring.

...with capable staff who are friendly.

...with continuity of care.

...to be respected and honoured.

...to be valued and listened to.

...with enjoyable conversations.

...with provision to meet your care needs.

...to welcome family and friends for visits.

...with good health.

...with privacy.

...with personal space.

...with a variety of activities.

...to pursue interests.

...with green spaces.

...to go outside.

...to go on outings.

...to have fun.

...to laugh.

...to appreciate the staff.

...with sensitivity to others.

...to know God has a purpose for you.

...to share your faith.

...to receive visits from people from local churches.

...to have fellowship.

Christmas blessing

"Look, the virgin shall conceive and bear a son, and they shall name him Emmanuel, which means, "God is with us."" (Matthew 1:23 NRSV)

Be blessed...

...with a time of peace.

...with a sense of release.

...to be able to ponder.

...with a sense of wonder.

...to know my presence.

...by being ever present.

...to be still.

...to know my will.

...to know my love streaming from above.

...with love so true.

...by being for you.

...with joy to savour.

...to know my favour.

...to know my care.

...with answered prayer.

...with delight.

...with a silent night.

...to know I am near.

...to know no fear.

...with my guiding light.

...to know my might.

...to live in my kingdom.

...with a sense of freedom.

...to live with me every day.

...with my son Jesus.

A New Year of blessings

"My times are in Your hands; Rescue me from the hand of my enemies and from those who pursue and persecute me." (Psalm 31:15 AMP)

As we enter the New Year and whatever it may bring:

Be blessed...

...in every area of your life.

...with God's joy and peace.

...by knowing God's presence with you.

...with enough to live and enough to give.

...with wonderful relationships.

...with the gift of being true in all situations.

...by knowing God's love for you.

...by seeing the good in yourself and others.

...by dreams come true.

May it be a year full of blessings.

Good Friday blessing

"But He was wounded for our transgressions, He was bruised for our iniquities; The chastisement for our peace was upon Him, And by His stripes we are healed." (Isaiah 53:5 NKJV)

Be blessed...

...that God loved the world.

...that God had a plan.

...that He gave His one and only Son Jesus.

...that Jesus died for the ungodly.

...that Jesus willingly offered himself for us.

...that Jesus bore our sins.

...to live for righteousness.

...that His death demonstrates His love for us.

...that by His wounds you have been healed.

...that we are saved from God's wrath through Him.

...that we are no longer God's enemies.

...that we are reconciled to God.

...to be saved from the consequences of sin.

...that Jesus knows what it is to be forsaken.

...that Jesus knows what it is to suffer.

...to be forgiven at the end.

...to have the assurance that you will be with Jesus.

...that it is finished.

Easter blessing

"He is not here; he has risen, just as he said. Come and see the place where he lay." (Matthew 28:6)

Be blessed...

...that this joyful day you remember Jesus rose from the dead.

...by God so loving the world He gave His only son so you can be forgiven.

...with resurrection life.

...with new life through Jesus.

...with the good news that Jesus has risen.

...by knowing God as your Father because of Jesus rising.

...by Jesus defeating death.

...with eternal life through Jesus dying and rising again.

...by the Holy Spirit living within you.

...by the Holy Spirit reminding you of everything Jesus said.

...by meeting with Jesus.

...by believing Jesus in your heart even though you have not seen Him.

...by celebrating all Jesus has done.

...by the Father and Jesus coming into your life.

...to ask the Father for things you need directly and receiving them.

...by Jesus returning to the Father's side,

...by Jesus leaving you the gift of His peace.

...by having great confidence as you rest in Jesus.

...by having the same power in you that raised Christ from the dead.

The blessing of the Holy Spirit

"May the God of hope fill you with all joy and peace as you trust in him, so that you may overflow with hope by the power of the Holy Spirit." (Romans 15:13)

Be blessed...

...by the Holy Spirit brooding over the void and dark ...places in your life.

...by the Holy Spirit comforting you.

...by the Holy Spirit being your advocate.

...by the Holy Spirit reminding you what Jesus has said.

...by the Holy Spirit uniting you with other Christians.

...by the Holy Spirit coming on you in power.

...by the Holy Spirit indwelling you.

...by the Holy Spirit giving you gifts.

...by the fruit of the Holy Spirit growing in you.

...to be anointed by the Holy Spirit.

...for the Holy Spirit to lead you into all truth.

...by the Holy Spirit birthing things of God through you.

...to be baptised with the Holy Spirit.

...with the Holy Spirit to speak through you.

...to prophesy by the Holy Spirit.

...for the Holy Spirit to give you revelation.

...to be led by the Holy Spirit.

...to be full of joy through the Holy Spirit.

...for your heavenly Father to give you the Holy Spirit as you ask Him.

...for the Holy Spirit to teach you what to say.

...to be taught by the Holy Spirit.

...with the Holy Spirit to testify about Jesus.

...for Jesus to give you instructions through the Holy Spirit.

...to speak in other tongues as the Holy Spirit enables you.

...to be filled with the Holy Spirit.

...with the Holy Spirit enabling you to speak the word boldly.

...to pray with others to receive the Holy Spirit.

...to be encouraged by the Holy Spirit.

...to hear the Holy Spirit speak to you.

...to be guided by the Holy Spirit.

...to have peace and joy in the Holy Spirit.

...by your body being a temple of the Holy Spirit.

...to know the fellowship of the Holy Spirit.

...to do signs, wonders and various miracles by gifts of the Holy Spirit.

...by prophesy originating in the Holy Spirit.

...to pray in the Holy Spirit.

Pentecost blessing

"But the Helper, the Holy Spirit, whom the Father will send in My name, He will teach you all things, and bring to your remembrance all things that I have said to you." (John 14:26 NKJV)

Be blessed...

...to be in one accord in one place.

...to recognise the significance of Pentecost.

...to thank God for the harvest.

...to thank God for His word.

...to experience a suddenly of God.

...to hear a rushing mighty wind from heaven.

...by the wind filling the whole house.

...by divided tongues of fire resting on each person.

...that that they were all filled with the Holy Spirit.

...to speak in other tongues as the Spirit enables.

...by hearing people speak your language unexpectedly.

...to be utterly amazed.

...to ask what does this mean?

...to hear the answer.

...to have an explanation.

...to be reminded of what God's word says.

...to hear how God will pour out His spirit on all people.

...that your Sons and daughters will prophesy.

...that your young men will see visions.

...that your old men will dream dreams.

...that both men and women will receive the Holy Spirit.

...that they will prophesy.

...that there will be wonders and signs in the heavens and earth.

...that everyone who calls on Jesus will be saved.

...to hear the good news.

...to hear that Jesus was resurrected.

...to believe that because God is with us, we will not be shaken.

...with a glad heart and a tongue that rejoices.

...to live in hope.

...to know the paths of life.

...to be filled with joy in God's presence.

...that God has all authority over death.

...to be invited to repent and be baptised.

...to be forgiven.

...to receive the gift of the Holy Spirit.

...that the Holy Spirit is for your children.

...that the Holy Spirit is for all who are far off.

...to be called to God.

...to be warned.

...to hear God's appeal.

...to be saved from a corrupt generation.

...to accept the message.

...to be baptised.

...that others come to faith.

Blessing of being God's child.

"The Spirit Himself testifies and confirms together with our spirit [assuring us] that we [believers] are children of God." (Romans 8:16 AMP)

You are blessed...

...to have God as your Father.
...that God is a good Father.
...to be unconditionally loved by God.
...to have God always with you.
...that God loves you as much as His son Jesus.
...to have Jesus as your brother.
...to share Jesus's inheritance.
...that God calls you His child.
...to be part of God's family.
...with numerous brothers and sisters.
...that God constantly thinks of you.
...that God knows the number of hairs on your head.
...that God watches over you.
...that God knitted you together in your mother's womb.
...that God's thoughts of you are more numerous that the
...grains of sand on the seashore.
...that God has good plans for you.
...that God gives you a hope and a future.
...that you have everlasting life.
...to be in dwelt by God's Holy Spirit.
...to hear God's voice.
...that God will guide you.
...that God forgives you.
...that God provides for you.
...that God protects you.
...that God inspires you.
...that God sees you through His son Jesus.
...that God sees you as holy and righteous.
...that God gives you His authority.
...that God anoints you.
...with every spiritual blessing.

...with an open heaven over you.

...that God draws near to you as you draw near to Him.

...that you are no longer an orphan.

...to know God.

...by God's peace.

...by God's joy.

...with all God has.

...with abundant life.

Blessing for the police

"When justice is done, it brings joy to the righteous but terror to evildoers." (Proverbs 21:15)

Be blessed...

...to be thought well of.

...with a good reputation.

...to be fair and just.

...to be unbiased.

...with good partners.

...to be appreciated.

...to have times of rest.

...with God's protection.

...with a sense of community.

...to create and live in safety.

...to be respected.

...with good friends.

...with good information.

...with good facilities.

...with wisdom.

...with good decisions.

...with God's provision.

...with insight and understanding.

...with time off.

...with good relationships.

...to look out for each other.

...with self-discipline.

...to treat everyone well and to be treated well yourself.

Blessing for those in prison

"God makes a home for the lonely; He leads the prisoners in prosperity, Only the stubborn and rebellious dwell in a parched land." (Psalm 68:6 AMP)

Be blessed...

...with a new beginning.

...with second chances.

...to turn your life around.

...to have righteous relationships.

...to have other people believe in you.

...to reach your potential.

...to see the good gifts you have inside yourself.

...to have opportunities to use these gifts to bless others.

...to have your mind renewed.

...to know God is with you.

...to know you are not alone.

...to know God loves you.

...to turn to God.

...by God's protection.

...with wisdom how to live.

...with making good decisions.

...to have job opportunities.

...with fellowship that loves you.

...to be a witness to all God does for you.

...to adapt to life on the outside.

...to have a home.

...to be directed by God each day.

...to know God goes before you.

...to enjoy spending time with God.

...to receive His blessings and share them with others.

Blessing for a school

"Jesus said, "Let the little children come to me, and do not hinder them, for the kingdom of heaven belongs to such as these." (Matthew 19:14)

Be blessed...

> ...to enjoy each other's company.
> ...to respect each other.
> ...to have a good reputation.
> ...with high standards.
> ...to excel.
> ...to be a place of safety.
> ...for everyone to be treated fairly.
> ...to have good discipline.
> ...to be a seat of learning.
> ...for everyone to achieve their best.
> ...with a welcoming atmosphere.
> ...with enough finance.
> ...with good facilities.
> ...with many friendships.
> ...to care for each other.
> ...to celebrate people's uniqueness.
> ...to create fond memories.
> ...to be somewhere for self-expression.
> ...with supportive parents.
> ...with being a friendly community.
> ...to support each other.
> ...to speak well of each other.
> ...with clear communication.
> ...to be a place of encouragement.

Blessing for a fire station

"and call upon me in the day of trouble; I will deliver you, and you shall glorify me." (Psalm 50:15 ESV)

Be blessed...

> ...with good training.
> ...with the best equipment.
> ...with supportive friendships.
> ...with a good community.
> ...with good teamwork.

...to look out for each other.
...to support each other.
...with enough finance.
...with great provision.
...with relaxation.
...with places to have fun.
...with good communication.
...with all you need.
...to be alert.
...to be aware of danger.
...with God's protection.
...to stay safe.
...to work as one.
...to be disciplined.
...to be appreciated.
...with good decisions.
...with wisdom.
...with understanding.
...with a good work life balance.

Blessing for a hospital

*"Praise the Lord, my soul, and forget not all his benefits –
who forgives all your sins and heals all your diseases."*
(Psalm 103:2-3)

Patients be blessed by knowing God's healing in your body.

Be blessed...

...by knowing His presence with you.
...with God's breath in your lungs.
...by knowing you are not alone.
...with God's shalom.
...all NHS staff
...with God's peace.
...by knowing God's love and grace.
...with renewed strength from God.
...with hope from the God of all hope.

...with perseverance.

...with peace and joy from God even in the difficult times.

...with the Holy Spirit hovering over the hospital giving

...order where it feels like chaos.

...by the Holy Spirit filling the hospital with serenity.

...with good hygiene.

...with teamwork.

...with enough staff.

...with correct decisions.

...with compassion.

...with understanding.

...with good facilities.

...with a good reputation.

...with all you need.

...to work in community.

Blessing for business

"Commit your works to the Lord [submit and trust them to Him], and your plans will succeed [if you respond to His will and guidance]. (Proverbs 16:3 AMP)

Be blessed...

...to thrive.

...with wisdom.

...with a steady income.

...with increase.

...with people who work well.

...with skilled staff.

...with good relationships.

...with times of rest.

...with enough work to survive.

...with good decisions.

...with good ideas.

...to be creative.

...to be appreciated.

...to succeed.

...to be part of the community.

...to treat others well and for you to be treated well also.

Blessing on politicians

"Let everyone be subject to the governing authorities, for there is no authority except that which God has established. The authorities that exist have been established by God." (Romans 13:1)

Be blessed...

...to fulfil God's will in the positioning you have.

...with strategy to bless those you serve.

...to enable good facilities for people.

...to help and support those to come to you seeking advice.

...to represent your community well.

...to listen and learn from those you serve.

...to work with those from all political parties for the common good.

...to live in integrity.

...to be respected.

...to seek God and find Him.

...to be kept safe.

...with support from friends and family.

...with a good reputation.

...with those who will encourage you.

...with creative ideas.

...to connect people to bring blessing.

...to speak for the voiceless.

...to treat all as equal.

...to make a difference.

...to influence outcomes.

...to see change you hope for happen.

...with perseverance to bring the breakthrough.

...to flourish and use all your good gifts.

...with a good homelife.

...to know that your times are in God's hands.

Blessing of comfort

"Blessed be the God and Father of our Lord Jesus Christ, the Father of mercies and God of all comfort, who comforts us in all our affliction, so that we may be able to comfort those who are in any affliction, with the comfort with which we ourselves are comforted by God." (2 Corinthians 1:3-4 ESV)

Be blessed...

...with comfort in times of distress.
...with God's presence as you go through grief.
...with supportive friends at a time of loss.
...to comfort others in the way you have been comforted.
...with hope.
...with seeing a future.
...with God speaking words of love to you.
...with reassuring words for you.
...to be able to adapt to a different way of life.
...with contentment.
...with good memories.
...to give to God anything you have concerns about.
...to know God's peace that passes all understanding.
...to know God's perfect love that casts out all fear.
...with a plan to move forward.
...to take one day at a time and receive strength each day.
...with encouragement.
...with purpose.
...with enjoyable times with others.
...to not carry any guilt but give it to God.
...to know you did your best.
...to be kind to yourself.
...to receive kindness from others.

Going deeper

Talk to God and see if He gives you any blessings. You may like to write/speak your own blessing for the nation etc. or write/speak a blessing not mentioned in this chapter.

Letter

Dear daughter,

You are my delight. I watch over you each day and I see the growth in your understanding of who I am and who you are in me. I go before you, and I will be your rear guard. When you call, I will answer. Invite others to call me too. As you do, many will be blessed by the way I work in their lives and situations. Selah.

Your Dad xxx

Prayer

Heavenly Father,
Thank you that you long to bless everyone and everything and we can share with you in doing this. Amen.

Blessing

May we be blessed to bless.

Books

The Father's Blessing Devotional by Wendy Thomas (2020)

Songs

The blessing with Cody Carnes, Elevation worship and Kari Jobe (2020)

YouTube clip

Father's Blessing, John Paul Jackson:
https://youtu.be/c5Nrgy1DGcg

Receive the Father's blessing

216

Chapter 9

Letters

The letters in this chapter have come from us both journaling around the Father's Blessing. Even though some of these letters start 'Dear Daughter', the message within them is also for sons as well. Each day there is a blessing from the Father's Blessing.

Day 1

I bless you to know me intimately as your loving Dad.

My dear child,

I am always blessing you in so many ways but the greatest blessing I give you is that of being adopted into my family. Even though you are my child you do not always know what it means to know me as your loving Dad. You think of me in many ways. All powerful, all knowing, divine. Too many ways to mention. Yes, I am all those things, and they are good things to be, but I had always thought you would call me Father and know me as your loving Dad. That is what I am, and I want you to know me that way. You know it in your head but that's not enough. You have to experience that relationship with me. I love you and I am always loving you. Nothing can separate you from my love. However, you will only know the depths of my love when you let me father you. I am the perfect Father from whom every father takes the name. I love you completely and I want you to experience my love every day of your life.

Love, your Dad, Almighty God

Dear daughter,

How I love you. I wait for moments when we can get together. You are never out of my thoughts, for you are my child. Listen and learn the language of love. Let me speak.

Let me help you change the way you think and how you respond to challenges and difficulties. There is no fear in love. Perfect love casts out all fear. Yes, ALL fear. It cannot stay when my love is there. Let down the drawbridge. Invite me into your day. Into all the joys but also all the struggles. For as your Father I will celebrate the precious times but be there to comfort and help when things happen that cause you pain or anxiety.

Love, your Dad xxx

Day 2

I bless you to know how precious you are to me.

My precious daughter, my precious son. That is what you are. My precious child. You are so precious to me I gave my son Jesus for you. There is nothing and no one more precious to me than Jesus but you are equally as precious as Him. I love you as much as I love Jesus. It is impossible to be more loved than that and my love is eternal. You are like the precious pearl that the farmer sold everything he owned for. Do not compare yourself to others because you are unique. I love everything about you as I am the one who created you. Yes, you are the apple of my eye. Receive my love and let it fill you to overflowing. It is a never ending stream and as you give away my love to others, I fill you with more. Be transformed by the renewing of your mind. Stop believing lies about who you are and how much you are worth. Let the truth that I speak to you and that you read in my word transform you. Simply believe. The more you do, the more you will feel my love and know how precious you are to me. I love you as much as I do simply because you are my child, and I am your Father.

Love, your Dad, Almighty God

218

Dear daughter,

You are so precious. Like a jewel that catches the light, as you let my light in, you reveal who you are in me. Others can then see your beauty. Those who I am working in their lives. Those who are seeking truth, seeking meaning. Others will want to snuff out the light in you because it exposes their own heart motives and agendas. Do not fear, for I am with you mighty warrior. As you are true. As you are you, I will move. I will move in your heart and move in the life of those you pray for. Those you journey with. Those you meet and they then go on their way. Yes, they go on their way rejoicing as you have spoken my word into their lives, and they have heard my voice and had a revelation of my love. Selah. Be still and know I am God.

Your tender Father xxx

Day 3

I bless you to know the full extent of your inheritance and know how to use it.

My dear child,

Yes, you share the same inheritance as Jesus, and it is vast. I want you to know everything involved, as it will change your mind set about so many things. Let's start with you own the cattle on a thousand hills. That makes you rich. Think about that. What difference would just that one fact make to you? But there is so much more. Everything I have is yours. I have blessed you with every spiritual blessing. Do not skip that. Read it again and let it settle in your spirit. Believe it, receive it, accept it. What are some of those spiritual blessings? Peace, love, joy, power, authority, blessings, favour, acceptance, forgiveness, grace, mercy, spiritual sonship and so much more. If you just went through that list and accepted each one and received it, your life would look so much better, so different. To use your inheritance, you first have to know what it is, then believe it is yours and receive it. Once you have it, you can live your life in the light of it. Think how different you would be if you received my peace and lived your life in that peace. I will help you know and receive your full inheritance.

Love, your Dad, Almighty God

Dear daughter,

Your reputation is not based on what you do, what you look like or where you live. You are my child, and your reputation is based on being true to who you are in me. You do not have to win the world, but let me win others through your life as you bear witness to my love and blessing in your life and heart. You are not to put yourself down but to value who you are. Loved, precious and positioned for a purpose. As you shine and radiate your belief and trust in me, others will take notice. Be still and know I am God.

Your Dad xxx

Day 4

I bless you to know you are joint heir with my son Jesus and that everything I have is yours.

My dear child,

I happily made you joint heir with Jesus, and I want you to know you are, as it will make such a difference. You can see all Jesus has and how He uses it, so it shows you what you can do. I gladly give you everything I have. I trust you and know you will use it wisely. You just have to realise ALL that you have. You cannot use what you don't know you have. Ask me what you have. Let me show you. Right now, you only know a few of the things you have, and you are not fully using them. It is just a nice idea to you that you have all that I have. You are not taking it seriously, as deep down it feels too good to be true. It is vast your inheritance which is why you need to write it down. You don't have to wait until you get to heaven to use it. It is for you to use right here, right now, while you are alive on earth. You only have to ask, and I will give you what you need. I always give you more than enough. I want you to have life in abundance. I want to give you more than you can hope for or dream of. You just need to receive it.

Love, your Dad, Almighty God

Dear daughter,

Everything. Yes, everything I have is yours. My abundant resources. As you spend time with me you begin to take hold of all that is available. Each moment you can receive blessing as you abide in me. As you learn, you realise what is important and what is not, and you let go and receive so much more. You hold to what matters. You persevere. You love against all odds. And you know my peace that passes all understanding.

Your Heavenly Father xxx

Day 5

I bless you to know you always walk in my favour and have an open heaven over you.

My dear child,

I love you more than you know. My love for you is vast, overflowing, never ending, big enough to fill eternity. Because I love you, you have my favour and an open heaven over you. This means you can use all heaven's resources and riches. Because they are mine, they are yours. You are my child, so naturally I share everything with you. How could I not favour my child? Of course, you walk in my favour. This means I will open doors that no man can shut and shut doors that no man can open. I will lead you and guide you and take you places that you could never get by yourself. You will meet people and know them in a way which you never could without my favour. Just let me guide you to where you should be. Hold my hand and walk in step with me. I will work all things together for good. It is a blessing to live like this with me. Things are so much better and easier. There is no good thing I will withhold from you. I am the giver of every good gift. I want you to live your life to the utmost.

Love, your Dad, Almighty God

Dear daughter,

An open heaven is like an open door. You can come in any time. It is open 24/7. You can sit in my presence. You can pour out your heart to me. I am not a distant Father. I draw near as you draw near to me. I embrace. I see. I listen. Let us spend time together. Though your sins are as scarlet they shall be white as snow. Talk about the things on your heart with me and I will talk about the things on my heart with you. In the exchange you will be changed. You will come to know that which is important and how to live a life of love.

Your Father xxx

Day 6

I bless you to know my goodness and mercy and experience them every day of your life.

My dear child,

My goodness and mercy will follow you every day of your life and I want you to experience them every day. Knowing my goodness and mercy is different to knowing about them. Experiencing them means you truly know them. My mercy is part of my forgiveness and every day there are reasons for me to forgive you. It is not a one-off experience when you become a Christian. It enables me to show you my goodness. My goodness is part of me and part of the root of my personality. I am love, and goodness is a demonstration of my love. All good gifts come from me, and I always work things together for good because I love you. I long to show you my goodness and mercy and for you to experience them. I always think of ways you can know my love for you and knowing my goodness and mercy is one of those ways. As you live your life experiencing my goodness and mercy each day, you will become more and more secure in my love and look for the ways I am showing you my goodness. You will be able to trust me and believe in me in greater measure. You will be wrapped in my love.

Love, your Dad, Almighty God

Dear child,

I will not snuff out a flickering wick. I will not crush a bruised reed. When you are fragile, I handle with care. With care and love you can recover. You can flourish. You can be strong, confident in who you are in me.

Your Dad xxx

Day 7

I bless you with success and to experience the fulfilment of your dreams.

My dear child,

Success is not something you have to strive for. Success is something I freely give to you. In the big picture, success is being truly who you are. The person I created you to be. Success is being happy about who you are and agreeing with me about who I say you are. Success is loving yourself and loving me and knowing how much I love you. Yes, that truly is a blessing, and one I want you to have. As you learn to love and be loved and be the person you are, you will be free to know what your dreams are and believe I want you to achieve them. Your dreams come from your heart, and I give you the desires of your heart. Yes, dream with me and know that with me nothing is impossible. Do not just know it in your head but know it as an experience, an everyday reality. Do not be afraid to dream big but if you want to start with small dreams first that's ok. As you experience the fulfilment of your dreams, you will be willing and able to dream bigger. Dream God sized dreams and I will fulfil them. Be honest about your dreams and together we will see them become true.

Love, your Dad, Almighty God

Dear daughter,

I have an inheritance for you that will never perish, spoil, or fade. Kept for you. No one will take it. There will be no dispute over it. It is yours and for everyone who believes and trusts in me. It will truly satisfy. You will delight in it. Yet even now I bring restoration. It may not look as you thought. It may not be as you planned, but you will recognise my goodness in the land of the living. Do not speak negatively, talk constructively. Let your words build up blessing so the enemy is not able to infiltrate, as that person is secure knowing they are loved. Let us take one step at a time. I know today you grieve but as you sow in tears, you will reap with joy. For the divine exchange always gives you more not less. I am here for you.

Your Dad xxx

Day 8

I bless you to achieve the desires of your heart for it is I who placed those desires in you.

My dear child,

You know that I put desires in you before you were born. I created you to enjoy certain things, to be good at certain things, to long for certain things. You do not have to be reticent in acknowledging your desires. As a good Father I want your heart's desires to become true. Talk with me and if you cannot think of your desires, I will remind you. They are part of who you are, and I think you are wonderful. You are precious to me, and I love you endlessly. There is no lack with me, so as you tell me your desires, I will help them come to pass. Nothing is impossible with me. I want you to thrive and have an abundant life and fulfil your destiny. If you achieve your heart's desires, it will not only change your life but those around you. There is nothing that you can dream of that is too big to achieve. I make a way where there seems to be no way and open doors that no man can open. Put your hand in mine and we can achieve the impossible. Live with expectancy and you will see your desires achieved.

Love, your Dad, Almighty God

Dear daughter,

Today I want to give you a gift. Will you open it? I have watched you try to guess what is in your presents. How you have shaken the parcel and listened. How you have felt the shape to try and determine what it is. Sometimes you have worked out what is inside. Other times you have had no idea. The gift I give you cannot be contained in a box or wrapping. It is the gift of sharing my love with others. You have already been doing this, but my gift will bless you and enable you to respond to what is happening around you, and in the nation and nations. It will ripple out in ways you could not ask or imagine for my kingdom purposes. I will open doors to share this gift and others will receive this gift for themselves. They too will go out and share my love, the kingdom will advance and others will come to know my love.

Love, your Heavenly Father xxx

Day 9

I bless you with my wisdom and to know what to say and do in any given circumstance.

My dear child,

The fact that you want my wisdom and realise how important it is, shows the start of wisdom in you. It says that fear is the beginning of wisdom, and you have that. Now you need to grow in it. Jesus is the personification of my wisdom, so as you learn of Him and grow closer to Him so you will grow in wisdom. Yes, my thoughts are higher than your thoughts and my ways higher than your ways, so spend time with me and learn of me. Be transformed by the renewing of your mind. Learn to think like me. You have the mind of Christ, so you can do this. I give wisdom to all who ask, and I anoint you with the spirit of wisdom and understanding. Read my word and your thinking will change. Listen to what you say, and it will show you what is in your heart, for out of the abundance of your heart the mouth speaks. I will show you what to say and do. You just need to be still and know I am God. The Holy Spirit will give you the words to speak when you need to.

Love, your Dad, Almighty God

Dear daughter,

See my love comes in like a tide but my love does not retreat. It covers, it cleanses, and it refreshes. Where you feel exposed, I say do not fear. Where you are concerned about the future, I say your times are in my hands. And, daughter, I am going to take the mirror in your hand that has become spotted and tarnished, that does not show who you are, and give you my perspective of who you are in me. When you hold this, you will flourish. When you pick up your own view you will wilt. Choose who to believe. Choose what is in your hand. As you do, your heart will be able to love and receive love. You will become all I have purposed, and you will be lost in wonder and praise. Because I am the God of more than. I do more than you can ask or imagine. Selah.

Love, your Dad xxx

Day 10

I bless you to be able to hear and recognise my voice.

My dear child,

I love being a blessing to you by just talking to you. I am so happy that you love hearing my voice and talking to me. Yes, you do hear my voice and I have said before my sheep hear my voice and follow me. If you stop worrying, you would know when it is me talking and when it is you. Actually, you do know, but you just second guess yourself because you cannot believe that I would give you your heart's desire and tell you things you want to hear. Yet you know I am a good Father, and if what you want is good for everyone involved why would I not give it to you? There are times of course when I have to discipline you and say things you don't want to hear, but even then, if you do what I say, it will all work out well in the end. I know you know that, but sometimes you need to be reminded. My plans are to prosper you and give you a future and a hope. Sometimes you think I am quiet and not talking but that is only when other things crowd me out of your consciousness. I will always talk to you, and you will always hear me.

Love, your Dad, Almighty God.

Dear daughter,

I know your struggles. The times when you are fearful. I long that you be full of my love and that all fear would go. I know when you feel you need to protect yourself by trying to work out those around you. Yes, be wise but let me protect you. I will guard what is precious and you will not lose who you are to become something you were never meant to be. As you bless others, shadows are lit up and colour will come to the greyness. As you bless others, offence has nowhere to latch on and you are free to go and hang out with them. There are no places you cannot go because there are no walls of hostility to keep you out. And you shall hear as you walk each day. You shall be instructed, and you will know where to walk and when. I love you. As you receive these words everything will change.

Your loving Father xxx

Day 11

I bless you with the ability to hear me guide you and to follow my directions.

My dear child,

I am always with you and talking with you. Sometimes the noise of your everyday life drowns me out, so you need to come aside and listen to me. You will hear a voice in your ear saying this is the way walk in it. I will tell you when to turn to the left or the right just like an inner sat nav. I want to be the one who guides you and you will be most fulfilled when you follow my directions. I will provide you with all you need to do as I ask you. Nothing is impossible with me, and I will make a way where there seems to be no way. You have the ability to hear me guide you. I will tell you great and wonderful things you do not know. You have the mind of Christ so you can think my thoughts and follow me. I will never leave you nor forsake you. I uphold you with my right hand. I keep you in safety and keep you from stumbling. I will not let you fall. Put your hand in mine and we will walk through life together. I love you.

Love, your Dad, Almighty God

Dear child,

My door is always open. I do not lock it. You are welcome any time. I am not an austere father. A distant father. I love to be close, to be involved and to be invited into your day.

Your Almighty Dad

Day 12

I bless you with my protection and send my angels to guard you.

My dear child,

I will always protect you and I will never let you down. I am your rock, your shield, your strong tower, and you can run to me when you are in danger. Sometimes I will send angels to protect you. Other times I myself will protect you. I have so many ways to protect and nothing is impossible for me. I make a way where there is no way. Sometimes I protect you and you don't even know you needed my protection. I am always with you, so I am aware of any danger that you are in. I love the way you rely on me for protection. You have no need to be afraid. I will step in and fight your battles for you. All you need is to be still for the battle is the Lords. Watch as I win you the victory. I am the good shepherd who looks after His sheep. If you are in danger, I will rescue you. Turn to me as soon as you need help, and I will rush to your aid. Do not be afraid.

Love, your Dad, Almighty God

Dear daughter,

There is no other person like you. You are totally unique. How I have longed to gather you in my arms in times of abandonment. There has been an assignment on your life, but this is null and void as you abide in my presence and let my light expose enemy strongholds so they can be dealt with. Arise and shine. Your light has come. My love lives in your heart, and as you get to know how much I care for you this light will spread. It will not be contained but will be seen by others and you will be my witness unto the end of the world. Selah.

Your Dad xxx

Day 13

I bless you with courage to face whatever circumstances you find yourself in.

My dear child, I know how life shows you so many situations and how things constantly change so I am giving you the courage to face each and every circumstance. I am in control of things and as your Father I want only the best for you, knowing that you have no reason to fear. You know me and you know that I love you, so you know that you can face everything unafraid. There are still so many things that are an adventure for you to experience but some of them look scary. All you need to do is put your trust in me and you won't be scared, and then you and I can go on some wonderful adventures together. I will work all things together for good so you can be courageous and tackle the difficult things instead of trying to avoid them. Life will be so much more fun when you tackle the things you don't like the look of. I will fight for you and protect you so you can relax and enjoy life, knowing with me you will be able to overcome everything.

Love, your Dad, Almighty God

Dear daughter,

When you make yourself vulnerable and speak the truth in love, I work in you and through you. When you have nothing left but your belief and trust in me, my abundance is there. Others see and hear and respond. It is time to mine. To go into the darkness and labour for the diamonds in the dirt. As my Holy Spirit works, the hardness that covers these precious ones will be broken through. It will fall away to show the beauty of lives surrendered to me. Miners do not work alone. They need to come up higher to rest and recover, for the grime of the day to be washed off. To bring a heavenly shift you need to join the shift for my kingdom purposes. Selah.

Your Dad xxx

Day 14

I bless you with my peace and joy.

My dear child,

I give you my peace in all situations. My peace is not like the world's peace in that it isn't dependent on circumstances.

In fact, the worse the circumstance the more my peace is noticeable. When everyone else is anxious, you can be at peace knowing that I am in control and by your side. The same is true of my joy; it isn't the same as happiness but is a deep down contentment, knowing that nothing is too hard for me to handle. My joy can be experienced in both hard and easy times. It comes from knowing me and is not dependent on what is happening. My joy is found in relationship with me. I give you my peace and joy freely and the more you experience them the more you will realise what a great blessing they are. As you get to know me more and more and you experience my love in increasing measure, the more you will know my peace and joy. The greater your trust in me the easier it will be to experience my peace and joy in all circumstances.

Love, your Dad, Almighty God

Dear daughter,

I know it has been busy for you. And I know at times it has not been easy. But you have stepped out and I will bless you, bless the work of your hands and bless what is on your heart that has not yet been realised. Selah. I delight in these moments. I love it when we sit together and chat. I will help you when you feel overwhelmed. I will protect you when you feel vulnerable, and I will enable you because those I call I equip. Selah. Your symphony has reached a crescendo. Where all that has been before informs the sound that emphasises the beauty of what you say and do. For what was done in the back story is now to come to the fore, not to expose you but to revive others and help them encounter me in the everyday and ordinary, in the challenge and brokenness, in their waywardness and ignorance. Selah. You shall go out with joy and be led forth in peace. I look forward to spending time with you.

Your Dad xxx

Day 15

I bless you with my perfect love which gets rid of all fear.

The blessing of spending time with the Father.

My dear child,

I want to know my perfect love to the very depth of your being. I want you to experience it every day of your life. I want you to be so secure in my love that nothing can shake you. Because I love you so much, I bless every single area of your life and I am sure that nothing can harm you. You are walking under an open heaven and my hand of favour rests on your life. Things are stacked in your favour, and you cannot help but have a good outcome. That does not mean that you do not go through trials and troubles. It means that everything works out well eventually. I work all things together for good. Where things are impossible, I find the solution for you. Nothing is impossible for me. You are never alone for I am always with you. I will never leave you. My love is an eternal love and will never end. My love is indestructible, and I love you outrageously and unconditionally. My love surrounds you and fills you, so you have nothing to fear.

Love, your Dad, Almighty God.

Dear daughter,

Perfect love casts out ALL fear. I know you worry about the next months and years. Take each day with me. Let love rule and fear will not be able to have its ways. You ask what does fear do? It robs you of the enjoyment of the present. It causes you to react to the unknown rather than respond to the reality. It oppresses your mind. It torments and it is hard to think out of the box and be creative. It stops you doing what you ought because of the fear of what may happen. You though, my child, I call to live in your freedoms. What are these you ask? To be blessed by each sunrise and each sunset. To be free to learn, to listen and to let go of all fear.

232

To be open to the leading of my Holy Spirit. To sing in your home and to speak blessings. To pray and seek my face. To believe and trust in me. Selah. To not limit yourself by your perceptions but operate from your identity in me where all things are possible. Let me teach you the language of love that will bring down walls of hatred, not through compromise but through your trust in me. That I am bigger and that the battles are not with people. Selah. It is time to fight in stillness, in quietness and trust. To stop boasting and judging. To lay indignation at the cross. Look to my focus. What do I require of you? To walk humbly and love justice.

Your loving Father xxx

Day 16

I bless you to know my plans for your future are for your good and full of hope.

My dear child,

You make my heart rejoice when I see your trust in me and your belief that my plans for you are for your good and full of hope. I love it when you take me at my word and believe me. It makes it easy when you receive my blessing with heart wide open. I love blessing you and love to see the effect my blessing has in your life. Thank you for believing me and receiving my blessings. The second part of your life will be even better than the first as you learn to trust me in increasing measure and receive my blessings. Life with me is an abundant life. Full of hope even in the difficult times. Nothing can shake you when you simply believe my words. I am your Father and as such I will always love and protect you and be with you. Nothing can separate you from my love. Because nothing is impossible for me you will always have hope, as you know I am working things out for you.

Love, your Dad, Almighty God

Dear daughter,

Do not be afraid. I am with you. From the rising of the sun to the going down of the same. Through the watches of the night. Fear not, for I will keep you. I will uphold you by my right hand for I am mighty to save. I will silence those who oppose you. I will correct and direct. I will not be mocked. I will lead you in the way you should go. I will give you the words to speak and the words to write. I will put people with you, and you will be put with others for my kingdom purposes. For I love you with an everlasting love. My kindness will lead you to repentance. And as you hunger and thirst for righteousness you will be satisfied. I have not forgotten your past. How you laid it down. I have not forgotten the battles and the bruising. Yet this I call to remembrance, your tender heart, and it is this tenderness that is so precious as you respond to my love and let me work in your life. It is time to restore wonder. It is time to bless you. Receive your Father's blessing from head to heart to feet. Selah

Love, your Dad xxx

Day 17

I bless you to know my comfort in times of trouble.

My dear child,

I always want you to know my comfort and then you will always be able to comfort others in the same way. You have to accept my comfort though. Do not so get caught up in the grief and pain that you cannot be comforted. Do not let the things that are hurting you define you. Lift your eyes higher and focus your gaze on me and my kingdom. As you do, the things of earth will fade, and you will become enraptured by me. You can't think and focus on good things and be in pain. My comfort comes in many different ways, so look out for the comfort I am offering you. Do not become trapped in the trouble. You are not meant to be trapped by anything. I have set you free for a life of freedom. Spread your wings and fly.

Do not let yourself be put in a box or your vision become so small you cannot breathe. My comfort is a blessing because it always comes in different ways and cannot be defined or contained. It is never ending and expands to cover every situation, no matter how big or how small. Nothing is impossible with me. I will see you through.

Love, your Dad, Almighty God

Dear daughter,

Place your hand over your heart. I have placed my hand on your life. I am working in your heart. Feel the reassurance, know it is real. Know you are loved. That you are lovely. That as you receive my love it goes out. Do not fear. I am with you mighty warrior. Do not be a mighty worrier. Stand in the armour. The truth is you are loved. The knowledge that you are saved. The assurance of your faith. The authority you have to speak my word. The ability to go wherever I send you. And you will be more than able to outwit the enemy's schemes and devices. Selah

Love, your Dad xxx

Day 18

I bless you to know my encouragement.

My dear child,

It is my joy to encourage you and I do that every day all through the day. You are easy to give encouragement to as you hear me and respond. I tell you things to encourage you and help you persevere. Things are not always easy but with my encouragement you can get through them. I encourage you in so many ways. In fact, I am your greatest encourager. My plans for you are to give you a future and a hope. My hand of blessing is on your life, and I work all things together for good. I will give you eyes to see and ears to hear my encouragements and wisdom to respond. Nature itself is my encouragement to you and I know how you appreciate the beauty of nature. Sunrises and sunsets, the sea, mountains, lakes, flowers, trees, so many things encourage you. Rainbows remind you of my promises and can encourage you. I have promised you so many things and I always keep my promises. I have told you that I love you and I will never leave you and I do not lie. These things should alone be my encouragements but there are so many more given because I love you and you are mine.

Love, your Dad, Almighty God

Dear daughter,

I am with you. Do not fear. I have heard your cry and I know your heart's desire. Be still and know I am God. Follow the leading and guiding of my Holy Spirit.

Your Dad xxx

Day 19

I bless you to know how special you are and all the good things I have put inside you.

My dear child,

My heart is full of love for you, and I am so proud of you. You are so special, so unique and you were created by me. You are everything I hoped you would be, my beloved child. It makes me so happy to know you love me and want to live as my child and have me as your Father. I will never let you down. I am always here for you. I have put so many good things inside you. Things you haven't discovered yet or don't believe about yourself. Learn to listen to what I say about you and believe it. You have listened to so many other voices, but they don't know you and all the good things inside you. Choose to listen to my voice above everyone else's. You are made in my image, so you are packed full of good things. You are a chip off the old block. Like father, like child. Live so that when people look at you, they see me. I tell you that with me nothing is impossible. I will tell you every day how special you are and how much you mean to me. I have so many good things in store for you. You have a wonderful future lived with me.

Love, your Dad, Almighty God.

Dear daughter,

You are special. You are loved. You are chosen. Every, I say every, hair of your head is counted. Do not fear man. What can he do to you? Let love be your plumbline. Your guide into the harbour. Let it light your path and be the rudder in your boat. As you do, you will see me work. You will see my goodness in the land of the living. Selah.

Your Dad xxx

Day 20

I bless you to know you are seated in heavenly places with Christ.

My dear child,

You are so precious to me, and I love you so much. I don't want to just bless you with blessings that make you happy for a moment, but I want to bless you with things that will make a difference for the rest of your life. If you truly know through experience that you are seated with Christ in heavenly places, you will be blessed for all your life. It will change so many things. You will be able to say clearly what is happening in heaven and do the same on earth. You will see heaven's answer to earth's problems, and you can take it with you back to earth. You will realise the authority you have. Problems will no longer be problems but opportunities to provide answers. You will be full of love, joy, and peace. You will know what I am thinking and doing and do likewise. You will know the language of love and blessing because it is the language of heaven. What a difference. What a way to live!

Love, your Dad, Almighty God

Dear Daughter,

There is another place. Not the one that is promoted by man but a place that is beyond your imaginings. Somewhere that you belong to, not because of your place of birth or language, but because you are my child. You will be blessed beyond all measure. When the place you know changes and the people you know do too, there is a place where you are kept, loved, and forgiven. AS you abide, others will want to know what is it that you have got. Selah. I delight in you my precious child.

Your Dad xxx

Day 21

I bless you to know all circumstances are under your feet, you're never under the circumstances.

My dear child,

I want you to know all circumstances are under your feet. I want you to have that confidence. It is a blessing I willingly give to you, but it is something you have to receive. It is a fact and a truth that all circumstances are under your feet, but you have to believe it to make a difference in your life. You are seated in heaven in Christ, and you cannot be any higher than that. That means that everything you see, feel and experience is under your authority. I share my authority with you, and you choose how things end up. When you truly know and experience this, it is a wonderful blessing as everything changes. I am in control even when you can't even see my hand on your life, so you can be secure. All you have to do is believe. Keep looking at me and your circumstances will fade away. Their importance shrinks as your focus on me becomes the main thing in your life. Listen to and believe what I say, and you say likewise. You will have the victory in every circumstance.

Love, your Dad, Almighty God

Dear daughter,

I know how difficult it has been with you. Yet as you trust in my opinion of you, and not what others think, you will flourish and blossom. You will be true, and you will see me at work in ways you could not ask or imagine. When you are disappointed in yourself, you can so easily miss all that is good, my grace and sufficiency to meet every crisis and redeem. As you trust in me, then the God appointments will happen. Selah.

Your Dad xx

Day 22

I bless you to be the head and not the tail.

My dear child,

Being the head and not the tail means you are victorious in all things. I am sure you realise what a blessing that is. You walk in my favour, and I open doors for you that no one can shut. The outcome is clear. You are victorious. You win as I fight your battles for you. Sometimes it may look as if things are against you but that is only temporary. I work all things together for good, so if it isn't good, it isn't the end. Being the head means you are the leader and decide how things should be. I give you my authority, for I know you will use it under my direction. I will show you the decisions to make for the best outcome. Listen to me and you won't go wrong. I will also close doors that can't be opened, as no matter how attractive some opportunities look, they won't end well. You need to trust me in this. As my child you will always win in the end and see things come together for good. Be full of hope and expectation.

Love, your Dad, Almighty God.

Dear daughter,

Did I not calm the waves? Did I not say do not fear? Did I not raise the dead? Did I not shut the mouths of lions? Did I not speak through a donkey?

Your Dad xxx

Day 23

I bless you with every spiritual blessing.

My dear child,

Be blessed with every spiritual blessing; is a wonderful thing but you need to receive the blessings. It is good that you ask what the blessings are, as you can't receive something that you don't know is being given to you. So yes, you are right, every spiritual blessing does include the fruits of the Holy Spirit. Love, joy, peace, patience, kindness, goodness, faithfulness, gentleness and self-control. It also contains the gifts of the spirit. Words of wisdom, revelation, gifts of faith, gifts of healing, words of knowledge, power to work miracles, gifts of prophecy, gifts of discernment, speaking in tongues and interpretation of tongues. They should be enough for you but actually there is so much more. I love showering blessings on you. I love you. Now listen, every spiritual blessing is found in me and my kingdom. I give you all of me and I give you my kingdom. I withhold nothing from you. Take that in. Are you feeling blessed beyond measure? I hope you are. Now it is up to you to receive the gifts and live in that blessing.

Love, your Dad, Almighty God.

My daughter,

When you are an heir, you understand that you will inherit. You have a promise, a hope, and a certainty. As you believe in Jesus, you receive everything that was planned and purposed for those who believe and trust in Him.

Your Dad xxx

Day 24

I bless you with every good thing.

My dear child,

Every good gift comes from me, so why don't you write a list of all the good things you have experienced so far. As you count the blessings you shall be amazed. Think of not just the things you have and the people you love but all the things in creation as well. They are all mine but given to you and others to enjoy. Then think what are the good things you feel I have not given you and are they really good? Maybe you think you should have more money. What would you do if you had more money? Maybe it wouldn't be a good thing? What if you had a bad consequence from choices made without asking my guidance because you had money. Would you still think it a good thing then? Your definition of good things and mine are different. My thoughts are higher than your thoughts and my ways are higher than your ways, so will you trust me? I am always willing to give you good things. You just need to ask and then receive them. To do that you need faith and to call those things that aren't as though they are. Ponder on that with me.

Love, your Dad, Almighty God.

My Daughter,

Intimacy is where your relationship deepens. It is knowing I am there through the good times and the bad. It grows as you pour out your heart to me and we spend time together. In moments when you sigh, when you laugh, when you sigh, when you cry, when you express how you feel. It is also there when you are not able to say a word, but you are simply aware that I am there with you. For I am your loving Father. Here to counsel, care, advise and embrace.

Your Dad xxx

Day 25

I bless you with a life of abundance.

My dear child,

An abundant life looks like different things to different people. To me, abundant life means no lack in any area of your life. It means a person is content and satisfied in every area of their life. Not only is their life on earth good but they have the promise of eternity with me. In fact, the basis of abundant life is based on their relationship with me. If someone knows me as their Saviour, Father and friend and they have full trust in me, they are content and secure emotionally, mentally, spiritually, and physically. Their relationship with me is the foundation of the rest of their life. As a good Father I supply every need and I give good gifts. In fact, all good gifts come from me. Having their basic needs met of being loved, wanted, cared for, provided for, and knowing they have a purpose and identity, they are already living an abundant life. As I did with my son Jesus, I freely tell you that I love you, you are my child, and I am pleased with you. You need nothing else. Be content in my love and enjoy your life.

Love, your Dad, Almighty God.

Dear daughter,

Where can you go where I am not with you? As you journey, I travel alongside. As you ask questions, I answer. As you seek me, I speak. I will not be silent, for I am a jealous God. I long that my people are blessed. If they do not receive from me, they will look elsewhere. Some already have but I say enough. It is time to build a beacon of blessing to draw them back to me. How do you do this, you ask. You build your beacon in the high places above all circumstances that would cause you to not do so. You build it through your relationship with me. As you allow my love to bless you, then you light up, you glow. And it is this beacon that is visible to all. What you have, you share, and you speak what the Father has given you. You speak the language of love and blessing.

Your Dad xxx

Day 26

I bless you to live a life of health and vigour.

My dear child,

Thank you for recognising your responsibility in order to live a life of health and vigour. If you listen to me, I will show you things to do to improve your health and vigour. Also, I have given medical personnel the skills to treat illnesses, so listen to them also. I keep you clear of accidents and illnesses far more than you realise. Also, there are times when I step in and supernaturally heal you. Yes, a life of health and vigour is a great blessing. You know the things you need to improve your heath and vigour, so do them. I will help you and encourage you along the way. I am always close to you to help you achieve these things. Be thankful for the measure of health and vigour you already have. Take times of regular rest and stop worrying. You have me as your Father, so you have nothing to worry about. I will take care of you and provide for you and keep you safe. Rest in my love and you will be refreshed.

Love, your Dad, Almighty God

Dear daughter,

You were overwhelmed and this is why you could not write. But I will restore the moments lost. I have a restoration plan. You will display my glory. Yield to me. As you do, you will not be disappointed for this is an appointed hour to release words of love and blessing to help those who are in despair, who are lonely, who have lost hope.

Your Dad xxx

Day 27

I bless you with renewed strength as you wait on me.

My dear child,

I said that your strength is renewed as you wait on me. That is indeed a blessing, and it is yours for the taking. You simply have to receive my love and know that I am in control and wait for me to act. You need to trust in my timing. I am always on time, never early, never late. If you believe this, you will be at rest. If your heart is entwined with mine, you will know my heart beats for you. You will also know that I am working all things together for good and so you can be at perfect peace. Can you imagine how much stronger you would feel if you never worried about anything. Think about the difference that would make if you were truly waiting on me, then this would be a reality for you. You know the truth of me being more than capable of acting on your behalf and sorting things out, but as yet it is not a full blown reality. It is the head knowledge rather than an experience. Let me show how I take care of you, and you will wait in eager expectation.

Love, your Dad, Almighty God

Dear daughter,

When you are silent, I continue to speak. Each day the sun rises. Creation shouts that I live. Each flower, each mountain, each valley, each creation, all display my glory. And you, my daughter, I created you and I care for you. I know when you sit, when you rise, when you lay your head down. When you praise. When you are active. I am familiar with all your ways. Nothing is hidden from me. I know you are struggling with this assignment, but I chose you and those I call I equip. I will enable you to be my witness unto the ends of the earth. Selah. I will give you the words to speak, the words to write.

244

All will be well. Do not strive. Be true. Be you. Today is a day of significance. Selah.

Your Dad xxx

Day 28

I bless you to know my rest and to sleep at night.

My dear child,

My promises are true and eternal. They may seem to take a long time to be fulfilled as far as you are concerned, but I will always fulfil them. I am not a man that I should lie. I am glad that you are enjoying my rest and sleep at night. Everyone needs that and they are a blessing from me. I love the way you are thankful for them. I will continue to ensure you sleep well at night. Yes, I will speak to you in dreams and help you understand them. I love speaking to you in all sorts of ways. As you are refreshed and renewed, so you will gain new strength. I am with you even as you sleep and wrap my arms of love around you. I set my angels charge over you to keep you safe. I love watching you sleep and seeing you totally relaxed. You feel my heart with love for you. You are so precious to me. I am so pleased you love me too. I am with you constantly and will never leave you. It is my pleasure to both meet all your needs and to bless you with all good things.

Love, your Dad, Almighty God.

Dear daughter,

I am with you today for I delight in you not for what you do but for who you are. I love the person. The character. The journey. The time we spend together. Selah. All will be well.

Your Dad xxx

Day 29

I bless you to walk day by day, hand in hand with me knowing the fulness of my love for you and knowing your worth.

My dear child,

I feel your excitement of walking day by day hand in hand with me. It is easy to focus on that and the positive emotions it evokes in you. I am glad you are excited by it, and I want you to continue in that. It is a blessing. I know you know my love for you, and you are right, you can always know and experience it in greater depth. It isn't that my love for you grows deeper. I have always loved you perfectly and always will. It is that you receive more of my love as you open yourself to me and draw closer to me. You can pursue me and my love the same as I pursue you. The more you know my love and drive out fear, the more you will know your worth to others as well as myself. Because of past hurts and rejection, you think others will not love you and won't truly love you and be good to you, but that is a false perception. As you fully know your worth in my eyes and the depth of my love for you, that will change, and you will assume that others will naturally love you and value you as I do.

Love, your Dad, Almighty God

Dear daughter,

I lay my hand of blessing on you. I know you are in unchartered water, but I will navigate you through. I know there are dangerous rocks ahead, but I will protect you and enable you to get to the quayside where you will unload what has been deposited, what has been carried, what is to be distributed. Do not fear, I am with you. I will insure. I will reassure. I will keep you through it all. Selah. For I am your mighty God. I am mighty to save. Who is it who enslaves? You will be able to remove your foot from the snare. All will be well.

Your Dad xxx

Day 30

I bless you to spend eternity with me and to know me fully.

My dear child,

I long for you to know me more. I delight in you and long to share myself fully with you. As you are ready to learn new things about me, I will share them with you. I rejoice in the way you seek after me and spend time with me and, as you do, you will know me more and more. I will hide nothing from you and share myself with you completely. Spending eternity together will be a blessing to both of us. I love you my child and I love spending time with you. I have so many things to show you about myself and my ways, and I know you will enjoy finding out more about me. I promise you the discovery will be of only good things, there are no nasty surprises. Trust me, both eternity and myself will fill you with joy. All that you have yet to discover will delight you and leave you with wanting to know even more. I will gladly teach you more of me and my ways. You have all eternity to know me fully.

Love, your Dad, Almighty God

Dear daughter,

I am so enjoying spending time with you. I love the moments we have together. They are precious. I remember each one. You are my delight. I delight in you. As you walk each day with me, I will speak. As you are attentive, I will attend to all that you are struggling with. Selah.

Your Dad xxx

Day 31

I speak blessing over every area of your life, not grudgingly but willingly, as it is my pleasure to bless you.

My dear child,

Yes, my Father's blessing shows my Father's love, and both are eternal. Thank you for being grateful for them. That touches my heart and shows you know me. Ponder a moment, and dwell on what your life can look like if you live in my Father's love and blessing. That is how you were always meant to live. Living a life of love and blessing. As you know my love and blessing and live experiencing them, so you too will want to love and bless others. Doesn't that sound wonderful? Why not start living like that now? I truly want to bless absolutely every area of your life. Nothing is too big or too small to bless. Everything about you is important to me. Everything is open to my blessing. Will you turn to me and ask me to know my love and blessing? It is a prayer I love to answer with a great big yes. I have always wanted to you to live a life full of my love and blessing. You just have to receive them. All my love always.

Love, your Dad, Almighty God

Going deeper

Start by praying and then write a letter to God. Talk to Him about everything that's on your heart. Then be quiet and listen and see how He responds to you.

Start your own Blessing Journal. Ask God how He wants you to go about making this personal blessings journal.

Prayer

Heavenly Father I want to have times when I have a father/child conversation with you. Where I hear your heart and you hear mine. I would like to explore writing you letters and getting a letter from you in return. Please help me hear you that clearly. Amen

Blessing

Be blessed to have daily conversations with God where He makes things as clear to you as writing a letter. Amen

Songs

Benediction (as you go) by People & Songs (2021) https://youtu.be/SFBw21E-yUI

Books

40 conversations that will change your life by Susan Franz Belisle (2021)
Letters from my Father by Wendy Thomas (2014)
From the Father's Heart by Charles Slagle (1992)

Final letter

My dear child,

I love you. That is all I want to say to you, over and over, in so many different ways that it finally sinks into your heart. I love you, I love you, I love you. You are my precious child, and I will always love you. Nothing can stop me from loving you and nothing can separate you from my love. I love you. Has it sunk in yet? I love you. I have always loved you. I love you right now this very second. I love you for all time in the future. I will never stop loving you. I love you unconditionally and mine is a perfect love that gets rid of all fear. I love you.

Do you hear me. Do you know how much I love you? You may think you know, but I love you far deeper, far greater than you can possibly imagine. Because I love you for eternity and perfectly, you can be secure knowing you will never be unloved. You are surrounded by love forever. You never have to be lonely for I am always with you. I will never leave, and I will never stop loving you. My love completes you. Because of my great love for you I bless you in every area of your life. You live in my love and blessing.

Love, your Dad
Almighty God.

Choose
Life

Enter in

Take hold of that
which I have called you.
Choose life. Choose love.
Choose blessings.

As you do you open the door
to others to experience
God's love and care for them.

About us

Wendy Thomas

Wendy Thomas was born and brought up in Southend on Sea, a coastal town in Essex, England. She has been married to Colin for over 35 years. They have four sons and six grandchildren, which keeps the family busy. Wendy has been a Christian since her early teenage years and the focus of her life is her relationship with God the father. Wendy was the National Prayer Co-ordinator for Street Pastors for almost 10 years. She is now the National Co-ordinator for the Father's Love and Blessing with the Neighbourhood Prayer Network.

Wendy talks at various venues around the nation. Prayer and the knowing God as Father message are the main subjects she covers both being very close to her heart. Wendy has also written various courses on the Father heart message which she presents at churches. Wendy has written 6 other published books and is a regular speaker in churches.

The books she has published are:-

> Walking with God as Father
> Knowing God as Father
> Forty Days of Love
> Our Father
> Letters from my Father
> The Father's Blessing Devotional

Lisa Hutt

Lisa Hutt was born and raised in Cheshire, in the North West of England. Lisa began seeking God as a child but became a Christian as a student in Plymouth. Throughout the years, Lisa's passion for prayer has grown as a result of her own encounter with God. Throughout her working life, she has served in a number roles including working for a prospective MP.

Lisa began working for the Neighbourhood Prayer Network in 2013 and is the longest serving member of the team. She currently serves as Director of Prayer, supporting a range of projects including A Mile with Jesus, London Prayer Loop and the Father's Love and Blessing.

Lisa has been married to Graham for over 27 years and they have two grown up children, one studying at University and another working in America. They have recently become proud parents to a cat named Angus.

To find out more and keep updated with the Father's Love and Blessing please visit:

www.thefathersloveandblessing.com

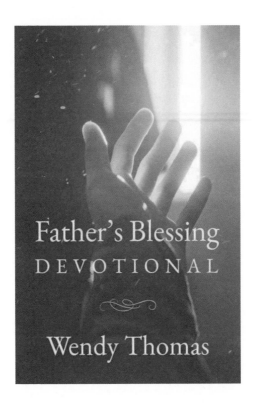

Father's Blessing
DEVOTIONAL

Wendy Thomas

From the very start of the book, Wendy takes us on a journey revealing different aspects of a loving Father in heaven who's heart is full of love for His children. Based on scripture and truth, she starts by laying a foundation of God as a Father who blesses. Then comes The Father's Blessing, a powerful personal message to each of us made up of Bible verses, laid out like a letter. There are 40 devotional blessings - messages of truth, each one based on a Bible verse. Don't rush through them or the short prayer at the end of each one. The impact of them comes from reflection and allowing the truth to bring life where you need it. There are other resources at the back of the book to help you in your life and those you love and care for. The truth contained in these pages has the potential to change your life forever and take your Christian walk to a new level of relationship with the Father of Love.